50
American Serial Killers You've Probably Never Heard Of

Volume Three

Robert Keller

Please Leave Your Review of This Book At http://bit.ly/kellerbooks

ISBN-13: 978-1535138406

ISBN-10: 1535138408

© 2016 by Robert Keller

robertkellerauthor.com

All rights reserved.

No part of this publication may be copied or reproduced in any format, electronic or otherwise, without the prior, written consent of the copyright holder and publisher. This book is for informational and entertainment purposes only and the author and publisher will not be held responsible for the misuse of information contain herein, whether deliberate or incidental.

Much research, from a variety of sources, has gone into the compilation of this material. To the best knowledge of the author and publisher, the material contained herein is factually correct. Neither the publisher, nor author will be held responsible for any inaccuracies.

Table of Contents

Francisco Acevedo 7

Lyda Ambrose 10

William Archerd 13

Anthony Balaam 17

Danny Lee Barber 20

Charles Anthony Boyd 23

Henry Brisbon Jr. 26

John Brooks 29

Raymond Brown 32

Eugene Butler 35

Billy Lee Chadd 37

Nathaniel Code Jr. 40

Rory Conde 44

Andrew Cunahan 47

Anna Cunningham 51

Robert Danielson 54

Bruce Davis 57

David Dowler 60

Jeffrey Lynn Feltner 63

Charles Floyd 66

Lester Harrison 69

James R. Hicks 72

Clarence Hill 75

Johnny Ray Johnson 78

Anthony Joyner 82

Steven Judy 84

James Koedatich 88

William Darrell Lindsey 91

Dorothy Matajke 94

John McRae 97

Bruce Mendenhall 101

Roy Mitchell 104

Henry Lee Moore 107

Eddie Lee Mosley 110

Francis Nemechek 114

Alfredo R. Prieto 117

Larry Ralston 120

Robert Reldan 123

Marc Sappington 126

Jason Scott 130

William Smith 133

Gary Taylor 136

Michael Terry 139

Louise Vermilyea 142

Alexander Watson Jr. 145

Dennis Duane Webb 148

Robert Wirth 152

Martha Wise 155

David Leonard Wood 158

Robert Zarinsky 162

Francisco Acevedo

In January 2009, Francisco Acevedo was pulled over in Brentwood, New York, and arrested on a charge of drunken driving. This was his fourth D.U.I. arrest and it earned him a one-to-three-year stretch at Green Haven correctional facility, beginning in May 2009. In January 2010, he completed an optional parole application, which required him to submit a blood sample for DNA profiling. Acevedo did this voluntarily, hoping to be released a couple of years early. Instead, he ended up tacking another 75 years onto his sentence.

Cold case investigators had been working the decades-old case for years. In that time they'd considered and rejected over 100 possible suspects. DNA evidence told them that the same man was responsible for all three murders, and yet the killer proved maddeningly elusive.

The murders had occurred in Yonkers, New York, over a six-year period from 1989 to 1996. Each of the victims was found naked, bound and strangled, posed on her back.

The first to die was 26-year-old Maria Ramos, killed on February 5, 1989, her body dumped near Ludlow Street bridge in Yonkers. Two years later, on March 28, 1991, another Bronx woman was found in the same location. She was 28-year-old Tawana Hodges, a known prostitute.

With the third victim, the killer varied his M.O. somewhat. Kimberly Moore, 30, was not a prostitute and her body was found where she'd been killed, in a room at the Trade Winds Motor Court on Yonkers Avenue. That was in May 1996, and despite an eyewitness description of the man Moore had been with, the case remained unsolved for 14 years, until Francisco Acevedo offered up his DNA and the police got a hit on the CODIS computer

The pudgy, middle-aged Acevedo made an unlikely serial killer. He was married with two young children, in steady employment and liked by all who knew him. Scratch below the surface, though, and a different picture emerged. Acevedo had a history of drug and alcohol abuse dating back to his teens. He had a lengthy rap sheet that included arrests for sexual assault, larceny, harassment and drunken driving. He'd served a 10-year prison term for the rape of a teenaged girl and had been released just 8 months before Ramos was murdered.

Neither was Acevedo the ideal family man he wanted to portray. A catalog of domestic violence arrests had seen him eventually sentenced to a year in jail for punching his wife in the face and breaking her nose.

Acevedo was arrested for murder in April 2010. He immediately admitted to having sex with the three women, thereby accounting for the presence of his semen at each of the crime scenes.

It was a clever defense but unfortunately for Acevedo, flawed in one respect. His was the only DNA found on Kimberley Moore, and the janitor who had found her body at the Trade Winds Motor Court, still clearly remembered Acevedo as the man who had shared the room with her prior to her death. It was enough to convict him of murder.

Acevedo was sentenced to 75 years to life in prison on January 17, 2012. As the ruling was read, he probably wished that he'd sat out the last two years of his D.U.I. sentence.

Lyda Ambrose

A "Bluebeard" serial killer is a man who woos and then murders a succession of female victims, usually for financial gain. His female counterpart is the "Black Widow," a deadly femme fatale who kills husbands, lovers, children, other family members, and sometimes acquaintances. One such creature was Lyda Catherine Ambrose. Born in Missouri in 1891, Ambrose used arsenic to dispatch five men, four of them her husbands, the other a fiancée.

Little is known about Lyda's childhood and upbringing. She first appeared on the radar in 1917, when at the age of 26, she poisoned her first victim. The unfortunate man was Lyda's fiancée, who in an effort to do the right thing and provide for her keep in the event of his death, took a $2,500 life insurance policy, naming her as the sole beneficiary. Not long after, he developed severe stomach cramps and died in agony, leaving her considerably richer. His death was attributed to stomach ulcers.

With indecent haste, Lyda redirected her affections to her deceased fiancée's brother, marrying him in Keytesville, Missouri, just days after his brother's funeral. He too was persuaded into taking out a $2,500 life policy, thus signing his own death warrant. Within three months, he was dead of symptoms that were startlingly similar to those his brother had suffered. The corpse was barely cold when Lyda was pestering the insurance company for her windfall.

Lyda now had a dowry of some $5,000, a considerable fortune in those days. But still, she wasn't satisfied. Moving to Twin Falls, Idaho, she took a job as a waitress in a restaurant and, within a short time, had taken the proprietor to her bed. The love struck restaurateur proposed soon after and the couple were married on June 10, 1918.

A month later he was dead. However, in her haste to cash out, Lyda had failed to ensure that the life policy was properly endorsed. It wasn't, and the $10,000 payout she'd hoped to gain came to nothing.

Unperturbed by this setback, she had soon snared a fourth victim, married him and sent him to an early grave within three months of the nuptials. This time, all of the documentation was in order and she walked away with a $10,000 check and the condolences of her deceased husband's insurers.

Lyda had by now perfected her little murder for profit scheme. Barely pausing to enjoy the proceeds of her last caper, she married husband number four in October 1920. The man expired less than a month later, leaving her the beneficiary of a two-week old insurance policy worth $12,000.

However, the insurance company was suspicious of the untimely death of a man who had seemed in such good health when the policy had been written just weeks earlier. They passed their suspicions on to the police and an investigation was initiated. A search of Lyda's cottage turned up enough arsenic-laced flypaper to ward off a plague of flying insects. Then, after toxicology tests turned up copious amounts of arsenic in her deceased husband's bloodstream, Lyda was tracked to Oakland, California, and placed under arrest.

Extradited to Idaho, she stood trial for first-degree murder, was found guilty and sentenced to life in prison. On May 4, 1932, she escaped from the Idaho state prison, remaining at large for nearly a year before she was recaptured in Kansas City, Missouri. At the time of her arrest, she was engaged to be married.

Lyda Ambrose was returned to prison in Idaho and remained there until her death, decades later.

William Archerd

Long before medical serial killers like Genene Jones and Donald Harvey became front-page news, a deadly Bluebeard by the name of William Archerd figured out a way of using insulin to dispatch troublesome family members and acquaintances. Born in 1912, Archerd showed an early interest in pursuing a medical career. Lacking the application to study for the requisite qualifications, he chose instead to become an orderly, and in 1940 found work at Camarillo State Hospital, in California.

Archerd did not allow his time at the hospital to be wasted, learning all he could about various drugs and their effects. He developed a particular interest in insulin, used at the time in shock therapy for mental illness.

In 1947, a close associate of Archerd's, William Jones Jr., died shortly after Archerd visited him in hospital. The cause of death was never determined, and no investigation was carried out.

In 1950, Archerd was arrested for illegal possession of morphine and sentenced five years probation. After a second offense, his probation was revoked and he was confined to the minimum-security prison at Chino. An escape attempt in 1951, saw him transferred to San Quentin, where he remained until his parole in October 1953.

Archerd had been free for three years when he married his fourth wife Zella in May 1956. Two months later, on July 25, he phoned the police to report a robbery and murder at his home in Covina, California.

According to Archerd, two men had broken in, held him and his wife at gunpoint, and forcibly injected them with some substance. The drug (which turned out to be insulin) had no effect on Archerd. Zella, though, had begun convulsing, then lapsed into a coma, and finally died. The men had taken $500 and escaped, leaving behind jewelry and other valuables. The story was bizarre, but the police somehow bought it, and Archerd was not charged.

In 1958, Archerd married again. Just two days after the ceremony, wife number five, Juanita Plum, was rushed to hospital in Las Vegas. She died the following day of symptoms that looked suspiciously like insulin poisoning. No investigation was launched.

Neither was any suspicion roused when 54-year-old Frank Stewart died in 1960. Stewart, a friend of Archerds, was hospitalized after a fall in an airport restroom (apparently as part of an insurance scam). That evening Archerd visited him in hospital. Stewart died during the night after suffering convulsions. Following his death, Archerd tried to press a compensation claim with the airport but was turned down.

At around this time, Archerd's brother Everett died in an accident at his job. Everett had entrusted $5,000 to his mother for his 15-year-old son, Burney. In August 1961, Burney was taken to hospital after supposedly being hit by a car (a subsequent investigation showed that no such accident had taken place). Archerd visited Burney at the hospital that evening. The following morning, the boy was dead, apparently from insulin poisoning.

William Archerd's mother (trustee of the $5,000 inheritance) died three weeks later, meaning that the money eventually went to Archerd.

In April 1965, Archerd married for a seventh time. His new bride was Mary Brinker Post, a well-known romance author. By November, Mary was dead, having been admitted to Pomona Valley Community Hospital in a coma. Her death was attributed to hypoglycemia.

Mary Post's death was one coincidence too many for the Los Angeles County sheriff's department, and Archerd was finally placed under investigation. He was eventually tried on three counts of murder. Found guilty, he was sentenced to death, although sentence was later commuted to life in prison. He died at San Quentin in 1977.

Anthony Balaam

A serial killer was loose on the streets of Trenton, New Jersey. Already, four women had fallen prey to the "Trenton Strangler" and police knew that if they didn't catch him soon, more victims were going to turn up dead. Thus far, though, they had very little to go on.

All of the victims were prostitutes, known in local parlance as strawberries, women who exchange sexual favors for drugs. Three had been found in vacant lots, the fourth in a room of a seedy hotel in a less than salubrious part of town.

The first to die was Karen Denise Patterson, 41, her strangled corpse discovered on October 24, 1994. Then on March 19, 29-year-old Valentina Cuyler was found lying among weeds and rubble in a vacant lot. Concetta Hayward was the only victim found indoors. Her body had turned up on April 10, less than a month after Cuyler's. Nobody at the hotel could recall who she was with prior to her death. Finally, there was Debora Ann Walker, found on July 29, 1996, in a vacant lot close to the other dumpsites.

Semen taken from each of the corpses proved that the same man was responsible for all four murders, but a run through the CODIS database came up blank. All the police could do was wait, wait until the killer showed his hand again.

The wait turned out to be longer than they expected. At the time of the Walker murder, the Strangler had appeared to be accelerating. However, he laid low for over seven months before killing again, and this time, he slipped up.

In the early hours of February 16, a woman was lured into an alleyway with the promise of drugs for sex. Once there, the 'john' produced a knife and threatened her. He then ordered the woman to disrobe before he raped and sodomized her. Somewhere during the encounter, the woman broke free and made a run for it. The man pursued her for a short distance before giving up the chase.

The attack was not at first linked to the Trenton Strangler. But after the rape kit returned a DNA match to the murder victims, the police eventually had a lead on the killer. They expected a quick arrest, but their quarry proved elusive. It would be nearly eight months before they had him in custody.

The suspect was Anthony Balaam, a 31-year-old, unemployed Trenton native with prior arrests for drugs offenses. Balaam made an unlikely serial strangler. Standing just five-foot-five and weighing in at 150 pounds, it hardly seemed possible that he had overpowered and murdered four streetwise prostitutes.

However, under questioning, the diminutive killer soon dispelled any such notions. Speaking in a soft voice, his speech peppered with "yes sirs," and "no sirs," he calmly described how he had murdered each of the women.

"He talked about rage," one of the arresting officers later said. "He talked about power, about his power over the women."

Anthony Balaam's case came to trial in January 2001 and resulted in guilty verdicts on all four counts of first-degree murder. The jury deliberated for 24 hours before rejecting the death penalty as an option. On January 26, 2001, Balaam was sentenced to life in prison without the possibility of parole.

Danny Lee Barber

Ninety-three-year-old Ruth Clowers had come to Huntsville, Texas, to watch a man die, had, in fact, waited 20 years for the privilege. Now, as she took her seat on the viewing deck, and watched Danny Barber being strapped to the gurney on the other side of the glass, her mind flitted back to the terrible day, 20 years ago, when she'd found the nude, beaten body of her daughter, Janice Ingram.

According to her killer, Janice had died as the result of a burglary gone wrong. Barber said that he'd previously done yard work at her Balch Springs home, and had decided then that he was going to rob her. He'd found a length of pipe in the undergrowth and had hidden it, intending to use it later to smash a window.

However, when he'd arrived to burgle the house, he'd found he had no need to break in. A door stood unlocked and entered through it. He was still carrying the pipe when he encountered

Janice. She'd started screaming, he said. He'd only struck her to shut her up.

But that didn't explain the number of blows he'd rained down on her head, nor the fact that she'd been found naked and had also been stabbed. 'I was drunk and I blacked out,' Barber said, using the age-old excuse of cons everywhere.

Yet, even if that were true, how does Barber explain his other victims: Mercedes Mendez, killed on January 17, 1979; Mary Caperton, stabbed to death on April 21, 1980; and another, unnamed victim, murdered on June 18, 1978. 'I was a different person back then,' is all that the Torrance, California, native could offer. Now he was about to pay the ultimate price for his actions.

The last time Ruth had been to the Huntsville execution chamber there had been a last minute stay. This time, though, there would be no reprieve for Danny Lee Barber. The intravenous tubes that would deliver the agents of his death had been inserted into his arms. Now, the gurney was tilted upward so that he stood, arms outstretched in a crucifix position.

"Hello, Ms. Ingram," he said (addressing Ruth Clowers). "It is good to see you. I said I could talk but I don't think I am going to be able to. I heard one of your nieces had some angry words. I didn't have anything to do with the stay. I spent the last twenty years waiting to figure out what's going on. I pray that you get over it and that's the only thing I can think to say. I'm regretful for what I done, but I'm a different person from that time. If you could get to know me over the years, you could have seen it. I've got some people over here that believes that.

"I want to talk to my friends over here for a second. Well, it's good to see you guys. Look after Mary Lynn for me. Like I said, I've called my mother already, so she knows. Okay, goodbye."

Shortly after, at 6:20 p.m., the lethal cocktail of drugs began to flow into the IV tubes. As the drugs began to take effect, Barber uttered a gasp and then was still. At 6:26 p.m. he was pronounced dead, dispatched with far less brutality than his victims.

Later, as Ruth Clowers and the other witnesses emerged from the prison, a woman down the street chanted her opposition to capital punishment into a bullhorn. All Ruth could do was offer a wry smile.

Charles Anthony Boyd

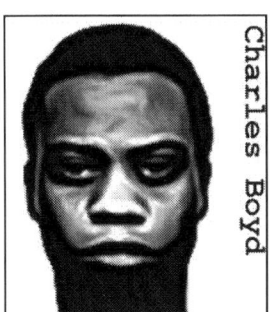

Over a ten-month period, from July 1986 to April 1987, three unusual murders occurred at the Woodstock apartment complex in northeast Dallas. In a series that the media dubbed "The Bathroom Slayings," the victims was strangled and then submerged in the bathtub. Each of the young women had been sexually assaulted. Two had also been stabbed.

The first of these horrendous crimes occurred in July 1987, when the decomposed corpse of 37-year-old waitress, Tippawan Nakusan, was found stabbed and choked to death in her bathtub. The body was badly bloated and it was estimated that it had been in the water for two weeks before the smell emanating from the apartment led to its discovery. Despite the chaotic nature of the murder, very little evidence was left at the scene. Investigators fully believed that it was an isolated incident. They were wrong.

That September another murder occurred at the Woodstock, so similar to the first that it could only have been committed by the same person. Lashun Chappell Thomas, a 22-year-old nursing aide, was found fatally stabbed in her bathtub. She'd also been strangled and sexually assaulted.

With the terrified residents of the apartment complex now on high alert, the common areas and hallways deserted, police began canvassing door to door. They turned up nothing that might lead them to the killer.

Six months passed. Then, on April 13, 1987, the killer struck again. Twenty-one-year-old Mary Mulligan was a recent graduate of Texas Tech University who had moved to Dallas to take a job as a management trainee with a local bank. On the day of her death, she'd stayed home with a sprained ankle. However, when she failed to answer her phone on April 14, her boyfriend called on the apartment and found her dead in the tub. She'd been strangled.

This time, though, police had a lead. Several items of jewelry were missing from the apartment and a bulletin to local pawnshops soon hit paydirt, when an ex-con named Charlie Boyd tried to hock some of the items. Boyd, who had only recently been paroled from a 5-year prison stretch for burglary and rape, worked as a night janitor. He lived at the Woodstock apartments with his brother. Mary Mulligan lived just across the hall, Tippawan Nakusan in the apartment above.

Boyd quickly cracked under interrogation and admitted to killing the three women. He was charged with all three murders but stood trial only for killing Mary Mulligan. At that trial, his defense attorney introduced the quite ludicrous motion that the charge should be reduced to voluntary manslaughter because, according to Boyd, Mary had called him a name. This was immediately refused by the court.

Another contentious issue was Boyd's competence. The defense contended that, with a tested IQ of 67, Boyd was borderline retarded and therefore not responsible for his actions. The jury rejected any such notion, taking just 10 minutes to pronounce Boyd guilty.

His request for a new trial denied, Boyd was eventually executed by lethal injection on August 5, 1999.

Henry Brisbon Jr.

On the night of June 3, 1973, a young woman driving along Interstate 57 in southern Cook County, Illinois, was forced off the road by a car carrying four men. One of them pointed a 12-gauge shotgun at her, ordered her to strip and then forced her to climb through a barbed-wire fence at the side of the road. As the terrified woman begged for her life, her assailant forced the shotgun barrel into her vagina and fired. Then after watching her writhe on the floor in agony for a few moments, he finished her off with a shotgun blast to the throat.

Less than an hour later, the gang stopped another car, this one carrying James Schmidt and his fiancée, Dorothy Cerny, both 25. They ordered the couple to get out and lie down on the shoulder of the road. Schmidt and Cerny begged for their lives, saying that they were engaged to be married in six months. "Kiss your last kiss, then," the man holding the shotgun said, before shooting them both in the back of the head. The gang then got back into their car and sped off, three murders having netted them $54, a couple of watches, and a diamond engagement ring.

Two of the gang members were arrested soon after, and it didn't take them long to give up the shooter. Henry Brisbon had pulled the trigger they said, committing the murders because he was a black Muslim who hated all white people.

Brisbon was eventually arrested and brought to trial in 1977, the year that the death penalty was reinstated in Illinois. However, because the murders had occurred while capital punishment was suspended in the state, there was never any chance of Brisbon being executed. Instead, he was sentenced to 1,000 to 3,000 years in prison. Ludicrously, though, he would he eligible for parole in just 11 years.

Given those odds, you would have thought that Brisbon would have done his time, kept his nose clean, and taken his chances with the parole board. Brisbon, though, had other ideas. Within the space of just over a year, he was involved in 15 attacks against guards and fellow inmates, had instigated a prison riot, trashed a courtroom and hit the prison warden with a broom handle. Then, on October 19, 1978, he launched a frenzied attack on inmate Ronald Morgan, stabbing him to death with a sharpened soup ladle.

Brisbon had avoided the death penalty for the I-57 murders, but this time, there would be no escape. In February 1982, he was found guilty of Morgan's murder and sentenced to die.

"You'll never get me," he shouted as he left the courtroom. "I'll kill again. Then you'll have another long trial. And then I'll do it again." It was a threat he'd almost get to keep.

Following Brisbon's death sentence, he was transferred to the Menard Condemned Unit to await execution. On February 15, 1983, he slipped his cuffs and attacked convicted killers William Jones and John Wayne Gacy with a sharpened strand of wire. Neither man was seriously injured.

John Brooks

Most serial killers get an early start to their criminal careers. So it was with John Brooks, arrested for the first time in February 1982, at the age of just 15. That arrest, for the molestation of an eight-year-old girl, landed him in juvenile prison, but if the intention was to teach him a lesson, it fell woefully short. Within five years of that initial arrest, John Brooks would be dubbed by New Orleans police officers, the "largest one-man crime spree" in the city's history.

By the time of his eventual arrest, on December 29, 1986, Brooks' rap sheet included two counts of attempted murder, nine armed robberies, one count each of rape, kidnapping, and attempted robbery, plus six murders – all of this before his twentieth birthday.

Aside from his juvenile arrest, Brooks first attracted the attention of New Orleans police on June 14, 1986, when he carried out a daring daylight armed robbery. Emboldened by his success he carried out another robbery on July 27, and another on August 23. This last robbery, though, was unsuccessful and Brooks took out his frustration by killing a victim, chosen at random. Fifty-year-old Wilbert Johnson was gunned down without motive on a New Orleans street.

Brooks was back to his robbery beat on September 1 and again on September 27, October 18, and October 19. Then, on the early morning of November 1, he committed another murder, shooting 51-year-old James Williams to death on a New Orleans street. Several witnesses described a heavy-set man walking up to Williams and firing at him without warning or provocation.

On November 27, a man approached taxi driver Artis Thompson as he sat in his cab. The man demanded money, but before Thompson even had the chance to reply, the assailant raised a gun and shot him in the head. He then robbed the cabbie's terrified passenger of her purse before walking casually away from the scene. The description provided by the passenger matched those given by witnesses to the Williams murder.

With a full-scale manhunt now underway, you might have thought that the killer would lay low for a while. He did no such thing. On November 29, he carried out another robbery. Two weeks later, he shot and killed Zachary Turnell as he sat in his car with a female friend. The killer then pushed Turnell from the car, drove the woman to a downtown motel at gunpoint, and raped her.

On December 20, Terry Young was gunned down shortly after leaving a New Orleans tavern and on Christmas morning a young couple was attacked and shot as they sat in their car. Diane Gipson died at the scene. Her boyfriend, Tyrone Wilkinson, took a bullet in the stomach but survived. Three days later, 18-year-old Darren Mercadel was shot down on the street as he stood talking to a female acquaintance.

By now, the police knew that they were hunting a serial killer, as ballistics showed that the same gun had been used to kill Young, Gipson, and Mercadel. And they soon had a suspect in custody, after a fingerprint lifted from Tyrone Wilkinson's car was matched to ex-con John Brooks.

Ironically, Brooks had recently come forward as a witness to a double homicide committed in October 1986. Thomas Morris and Cabrini Jareau had been shot while sitting in a parked car and Brooks claimed to have seen the shooter. As it turned out, he was not so much a witness, as the perpetrator.

Brooks was eventually tried for the Johnson, Williams, Thompson, Young, Gipson, and Mercadel murders. He was sentenced to death in 1991, but the penalty was commuted to life in prison in December 1997.

Raymond Brown

The murder scene was one of the most gruesome ever seen in Clay County, Alabama. Three victims, an 83-year old, her 63-year-old daughter and a 31-year-old niece, lay dead, literally torn apart, the victims of a vicious knife attack. They'd suffered over 100 stab wounds. In addition, the 31-year-old had been sliced open, a jagged wound running from throat to groin.

The best clue investigators had, was a bloody footprint left at the scene. It led them, after a two-week investigation, to a surprise suspect, the 14-year-old great-grandson, grandson and nephew of the three victims.

Raymond Eugene Brown was arrested and charged with murder. Tried as an adult, he was sentenced to life imprisonment, serving just 12 years before his release in 1973.

Brown had trained to be an auto mechanic while in prison and on his release he found work at a workshop in Ashland, Alabama.

In 1980, he was sent back to prison after he tried to rape the manager of his apartment building. When the woman resisted, he strangled her into submission and left her for dead. Fortunately, she survived and was able to name her assailant.

Despite his history of violence, Brown was paroled again in 1986, moving this time to Montgomery. In 1987, he began dating Linda LeMonte, 32, a divorcee with two young children. By all accounts, their relationship was stable. There were certainly no complaints of domestic violence against Brown. All of that was to change in August 1989.

On the morning of August 10, Linda LeMonte's supervisor called Linda's mother, Beverley Evans, to let her know that Linda had not shown up for work. Evans then phoned Linda's home and got no reply. Her next call was to her grandchildren's school – they were not there.

Concerned now, Evan's and her husband drove to Linda's house. When no one answered the door, Evans went to her grandson Aaron's bedroom and knocked on the window. The 6-year-old boy crawled from beneath his bed and ran to open the front door.

A scene of unprecedented carnage awaited Beverley Evans. Linda lay in the living room, multiple stab wounds to her chest, throat, abdomen and genitals. A 27-inch cut, running from her throat to her pubic region, exposed her viscera and abdominal cavity. Ten-year-old Sheila was in the bedroom, the handle of a knife protruding from her belly, the blade completely embedded. There was evidence that the little girl had also been sexually assaulted.

There was little doubt as to who had carried out the horrendous murders and a search was immediately launched for Raymond

Brown. The police also went public with his description, warning that he was likely to kill again.

Late on August 10, came a report that Brown's motor vehicle had been involved in an accident near Jordan Lake, some 20 miles north of Montgomery. A massive manhunt was concentrated on the area. Brown was captured 48 hours later, after he walked into a gas station in Wallsboro and was recognized by the attendant.

In the wake of Brown's arrest, the Alabama Board of Pardons and Paroles came under intense criticism for releasing such a dangerous felon into society. State prosecutors were not about to make the same mistake twice. Tried for murder in 1988, Raymond Brown was found guilty and sentenced to death. He awaits execution on Alabama's death row.

Eugene Butler

Eugene Butler went by the nickname "Eccentric," a polite way for his neighbors in rural North Dakota to say that they thought him a bit of a weirdo. Not only was the man a recluse, but he was also deeply paranoid. The few people who got to exchange words with Eugene reported that he constantly raved about the casual laborers he hired on his farm wanting to rob him. Eventually, his delusions overwhelmed him and in 1906, he was declared insane and sent to the asylum at Jamestown. He remained there until his death in 1913.

Few in Niagara, North Dakota, mourned or even noted Butler's passing. Little did they know that, within two years, old "Eccentric" was going to be the region's biggest story.

It happened in 1915 when workmen arrived at the Butler spread to renovate the farmhouse in preparation for a sale. The old place had fallen into wrack and ruin in the years since Butler's death and required extensive work from top to bottom.

After emptying the homestead of its contents, the workmen went into the cellar to prop the support beams to correct a sagging floor. As they began their evacuation, one of the workers disinterred a pile of old bones. Uncertain what they were, the men continued digging. However, after unearthing a human skull, all building operations were halted and the police were called.

A thorough excavation of the cellar eventually turned up six shallow graves, each containing the skeletal remains of a young man, estimated by the coroner to have been between 15 and 18 years of age. The victims had died of massive blunt force trauma to their skulls, and given the time span in which the murders were judged to have been committed, there was little doubt that the now-deceased Eugene Butler was responsible.

Yet that realization brought a raft of new questions. Who were the victims? Why had they been killed?

An investigation into local missing persons determined that the men were not from the area, leading police to conclude that they had been iterant workers on the Butler farm. That conclusion also pointed to a motive. Eugene Butler was always complaining of workers trying to rob him, so perhaps he'd caught them in the act, or had decided to strike the first blow before they could relieve him of his possessions. That sounded about right and was the official line adopted by the authorities.

Of course, the more obvious explanation was that "Eccentric" Eugene Butler was a prototypical gay sex killer, foreshadowing Dean Corll, John Wayne Gacy and Jeffrey Dahmer. Perhaps out of respect for the dead, that theory was never proffered.

Billy Lee Chadd

On the evening of July 26, 1974, 30-year-old Patricia Franklin returned to her Linda Vista, California, home and began to get ready for a date she had that night.

At around 7:30, she took a phone call from a friend and they spoke for several minutes. When the friend called back an hour later, there was no reply and he assumed she'd already gone out.

The following day, San Diego police were sent to the house after Patricia failed to show at work. They found her naked body tied to a bed. She'd been brutally raped and murdered, with fifteen knife wounds inflicted to her neck. There was also evidence of torture and one of her nipples had been nearly bitten off.

Four years later, on February 15, 1978, two Mira Mesa schoolchildren came home to find the bloodied body of their babysitter, 28-year-old Linda Hewitt, sprawled on the floor. The children quickly dialed 911, then waited outside for the police to arrive.

One of the officers sent to the scene was veteran San Diego homicide detective Bob Quigley. Quigley had also worked the Patricia Franklin case and although four years had passed since that crime, he immediately felt that the same man was responsible. As in the Franklin case, the killer had taken his time with Linda

Hewitt, his objective apparently to inflict as much pain and suffering as he could. Linda's throat was slashed, her spinal cord severed, her kidneys and back punctured by numerous stab wounds.

Several clues were followed up and Quigley was able to glean what he believed was a description of the killer. But the case was going nowhere until Louisiana sheriff's deputies, acting on an interstate fugitive warrant, arrested a young Marine corporal named Billy Lee Chadd, wanted for a double rape in California.

On March 2, 1978, a Chula Vista woman had awakened to find a man in her bedroom, holding a machete. Placing the blade to her throat he raped the woman repeatedly. Then, when her 17-year-old daughter entered the bedroom to investigate a noise, the intruder attacked her as well. He then tied up the rest of the family, including four young girls and the homeowner's parents. Then he bound and gagged the mother and daughter and drove them through Chula Vista to a remote area where he released them. A customs officer later found the women walking along a road.

Questioned by police regarding the attack, the elder victim reported that she'd seen the rapist around the naval base and was sure that he worked at the hospital. Detectives followed up on this clue and turned up the name of Billy Lee Chadd. However, when they arrived at the Imperial Beach home Chadd shared with his wife and 6-month-old child, their man had already fled.

Chadd was flown back from Louisiana to San Diego, where the two rape victims had no trouble in picking him out of a police line-up. He was booked on rape, kidnapping, and robbery charges and sent to the San Diego County jail to await trial.

While Chadd was there, investigators in the Franklin and Hewitt cases got to hear of his jailhouse boasts about those murders. However, when they visited the rape suspect in jail, he immediately clammed up and refused to talk.

Some months later, in December 1978, Chadd sent a message to detectives requesting a meeting. This time, he did talk, confessing to the rapes and murders of Patricia Franklin and Linda Hewitt as well as two others – a gay hotel porter in Las Vegas in 1975 and another, unnamed, man in Kentucky a year earlier.

Billy Lee Chadd went on trial for the murders of Patricia Franklin and Linda Hewitt in 1979. He asked for the death penalty and the jury took less than two hours to oblige him. On May 12, 1979, he was sentenced to die in the gas chamber at San Quentin. That conviction would later be overturned and commuted to life in prison without parole.

Nathaniel Code Jr.

Born on March 12, 1956, in Shreveport, Louisiana, Nathaniel Code Jr. followed the path of most serial killers, racking up a catalog of juvenile offenses. The surly youth then graduated to more serious crime. In 1976, he was convicted on a charge of aggravated rape.

That kept him in prison for eight years, during which time he was diagnosed as schizophrenic. That diagnosis notwithstanding, he was back on the streets by 1984. Soon he'd unleash one of the bloodiest killing sprees in Shreveport's history.

The first murder occurred on the night of August 30, 1984, when Code broke into the home of 25-year-old Debra Ford, tied her up with an electrical cord, gagged her, and then stabbed her 18 times. He then slashed Ford's throat, the blade cutting so deep that she was almost decapitated.

The murder was discovered the following morning. Code, who lived nearby, was one of those rubber-necking at the police barrier when Ford's body was removed from the scene.

Almost a year later, and just a few blocks from the Ford crime scene, another atrocity was committed. This time, there were four victims: Vivian Chaney, her 15-year-old daughter Carlitha Culbert, her boyfriend Billy Joe Harris, and her brother Jerry Culbert.

As in the Ford murder, Code gained entry to the house via an unlocked door. Once inside, he set about tying up and gagging the victims, using electrical cords and shoelaces. Then he systematically began dispatching his captives. The men went first. Harris was shot twice in the head, twice in the chest, and slashed across the throat. Jerry Culbert, who was sight-impaired and mentally-challenged, was killed by a bullet to the head.

The killer then turned his attention to the terrified women, sadistically forcing Vivian Chaney to watch as he slashed her 15-year-old daughter's throat. He then dragged Vivian to the bathroom, throttled her, and drowned her in the tub. Her two youngest daughters, aged ten and seven, were spared, although the girls, like their uncle, were mentally retarded and unable to shed any light on what had happened. The only clue that the police had was a report of a man seen running from the house, spattered in blood. That lead soon petered out and the trail went cold.

The police were no closer to solving the quadruple homicide when Code struck for a third time, on August 5, 1987. This time, though, he made a crucial mistake, killing three people who could be directly connected to him.

On the night in question, Code arrived at the home of his estranged grandfather, William Code. Code Senior was babysitting two neighborhood kids, Eric Williams, 8, and Joe Robinson, 12, that night, but it didn't stop Code carrying out the bloody revenge he'd been planning for some time.

First, he tied up and gagged the three victims. Then he beat and stabbed his grandfather to death before turning his attention to the young boys. Eric Williams was strangled to death. Joe Robinson was beaten and strangled. There was evidence to suggest that Code had tried to rape the older boy.

Unfortunately for Code, a neighbor spotted him leaving his grandfather's house, something that struck the man as odd, as the two men were not on good terms. He called the police, who arrived to find another massacre.

Nathaniel Code was picked up on suspicion of murder. Fingerprints lifted from the scene matched those found at the Ford and Chaney homes, connecting him to each of those murders. Once an eyewitness picked him from a lineup, as the man seen running from the Chaney house, Code was in deep trouble.

He was eventually tried for the four Chaney murders, convicted and sentenced to death. Decades later, that sentence remains under appeal.

50 American Monsters You've Probably Never Heard Of Volume 3

Rory Conde

The Tamiami trail is the nickname given to the final section of Highway 41, running from Tampa to Miami. For ten months, from September 1994 to June 1995, it was also the dumping ground of a serial killer known as the Tamiami Strangler.

The first victim of this vicious slayer was a cross-dressing male prostitute named Lazaro Comesana. His body was found dumped beside the highway on September 16, 1994. He'd been beaten and strangled to death.

Just weeks later, another prostitute, Elisa Martinez, was found discarded at the roadside. Like the previous victim, she had died of strangulation. There was also evidence that she had been sodomized after death.

Victim number three showed up soon after. She was Charity Nava, another prostitute, found dead along the Tamiami Trail on

November 20. And if the police had any doubts that a serial killer was responsible, that was put to rest by a message scrawled on the back of the corpse with a marker. "Third," it taunted. "See if you can catch me."

This latest murder had the police frantically scrambling for clues and increasing patrols along the trail. But while the police were busy, the killer was too, striking three more times over the next six weeks. Wanda Crawford, Nicole Schneider, and Rhonda Dunn were all found at the roadside, strangled and with evidence of sodomy after death.

Within weeks of the Dunn murder, investigators had DNA confirmation that the same man was responsible for all six murders. What they didn't have, was a suspect, and at the rate this man was killing there were genuine fears that he'd soon be into double figures.

But then, the Tamiami Strangler surprised everyone by suddenly dropping out of sight. No new corpses showed up between mid-January and June 1995. Had the killer left the area? Been killed? Been put away on another charge?

On June 1995, neighbors of a man named Rory Conde called 911 to report frantic banging coming from his apartment. Firefighters were dispatched to the scene and, after breaking in, found a naked woman, bound and with duct tape plastered over her mouth. The victim admitted that she was a prostitute and had been brought to the apartment to have sex with the occupant. Once there, the man had overpowered her, tied her up and then left.

The police were called and tracked Conde to his grandmother's house in Hialeah. He was placed under arrest and a subsequent search of his apartment linked him to the Tamiami murders. A DNA match, to semen taken from the victims, proved that the police finally had their man.

With the evidence against him, Conde must have realized that there was no point in denying his involvement. He soon confessed, saying that a recent split with his wife had led him to begin using prostitutes. His murderous rage, he said, was sparked after he picked up Lazaro Comesana. Realizing that Comesana was a man, Conde had snapped and strangled him, later dumping his body at the roadside. Thereafter, he'd brought five more prostitutes back to his apartment, strangled them from behind, and committed sodomy on their corpses.

On July 12, 1995, Conde was charged with six counts of first-degree murder. He'd face six separate trials, receiving life terms in five of them. In the sixth case (the murder of Rhonda Dunn), Conde was sentenced to death. He currently awaits execution at the state prison in Starke, Florida.

Andrew Cunahan

On July 15, 1997, the world was stunned by the murder of fashion icon, Gianni Versace, gunned down on the steps of his home in Miami, Florida. His killer, Andrew Phillip Cunahan, was already known to authorities and was in fact wanted in four other murders committed over a three-month period, as he rampaged cross-country from Minnesota to Florida.

Eight days after the Versace murder the serial (some would say, spree) killer was dead himself, killed by a self-inflicted bullet wound to the head. Which left the police and public alike to wonder; who exactly was Andrew Cunahan? And what had caused such an explosion of rage?

Andrew Cunahan was born in National City, California, on August 31, 1969. His father, Modesto, was a Filipino-American Navy vet turned stockbroker, and the family lacked for nothing. Living in the upscale Rancho Bernardo suburb of San Diego, Andrew attended the elite Bishop's School in La Jolla, where he excelled. He reportedly had an I.Q. of 147 and a near photographic memory. He was also a prolific liar and a desperate attention seeker.

After graduating high school in 1987, he enrolled at the University of California, San Diego. However, just a year later, his life was thrown into chaos when his father fled the country to avoid an embezzlement charge. Andrew was 19 years old and not about to accept the newfound hardship the family had been plunged into. Openly gay since high school, he became a high-class prostitute of sorts, a companion to a succession of wealthy older men.

All went well until 1996, when Cunahan was dropped by his latest lover. Almost overnight the self-indulgent, status-obsessed Cunahan went from a comfortable, glamorous lifestyle to a sordid, lonely existence. He began abusing drugs and his previously immaculate appearance became disheveled. To the friends that he still had, he'd complain that only one man had truly loved him, a wealthy Minneapolis architect named David Madson. Madson had ended their relationship due to Cunahan's involvement with drugs.

In mid-April 1997, Cunahan told friends he was moving to San Francisco. They gave him a lavish send-off before he boarded a plane the following day – not to San Francisco though, but to Minneapolis. He'd confided in a friend that he had "business to take care of" there.

Arriving in the City of Lakes on April 25, Cunahan had dinner with Madson before hooking up with an old buddy, Jeffrey Trail. On

April 27, Cunahan invited Trail to Madson's apartment, where he bludgeoned him to death with a hammer. Trail's body was found two days later, wrapped in a carpet.

Two days after Trail's body was discovered, Cunahan either forced or persuaded Dave Madson to drive with him to a lake about 50 miles north of Minneapolis. There, he used Jeffrey Trail's handgun to pump several bullets into the head of the man he'd once described as, "the love of my life."

Cunahan drove next to Chicago where, on May 4, he shot prominent real estate developer, Lee Miglin, to death. Five days later, he showed up in Pennsville, New Jersey, where he killed William Reese, the caretaker of Finn's Point National Cemetery. He drove away from the scene in Reese's red Chevy pickup.

By now Cunahan was on the FBI's Most Wanted List and a massive manhunt was underway to find him. Avoiding the dragnet, he headed for Miami Beach, Florida, where he lay low for two months. He re-emerged on July 14, 1997, to commit the murder that would grant him a fleeting notoriety.

On Tuesday, July 14, Gianni Versace was returning to his Ocean Drive home when a young man dressed in a white shirt and gray shorts approached him. The man raised a .40-caliber pistol, and fired twice, hitting the 50-year-old designer in the head. The shooter then fled the scene and dashed into a nearby parking garage.

It was there that police found the red Chevy pickup that had been stolen from William Reese in New Jersey. Inside the truck was a U.S. passport in the name of Andrew Phillip Cunahan.

With Cunahan's photograph flashed on every news channel, sightings were reported from every state in the nation. The killer hadn't gone far, though. Eight days after the Versace murder the caretaker of a houseboat, docked just 40 blocks from Versace's home, noticed signs of a break-in. The man rushed off to call the police, who arrived within minutes. In the upstairs bedroom of the vessel lay Andrew Cunahan, killed by a single bullet wound to the head.

Anna Cunningham

Anna Cunningham was a prolific poisoner who committed her crimes first at the family farm in Bachley Corners, Indiana, and later in Gary, Indiana. The victims were members of her family and the motive financial. Yet Cunningham insisted that she killed her children in order that they might "join their father in heaven."

She omitted to mention that she'd sent him there herself, with one of her arsenic-laced sandwiches.

David Cunningham, Anna's husband, had died in 1919, after enduring several days of agonizing stomach pains. Ever the dutiful wife, Anna had nursed him through his illness then made funeral arrangements and collected $1,000 on his life insurance.

With her husband in the ground and none of her children inclined to take up the farming vocation, Anna decided to put the family farm on the market. She realized $4,000 from the sale to her neighbor. Flush with her windfall, she relocated her family to the city of Gary.

A year after their arrival, Anna's 28-year-old daughter, Isabelle, succumbed to similar symptoms to those of her father. Anna cashed in on a $1,000 policy, taken out just five weeks before Isabelle's death.

The next to die was Harry, 23. His passing, in 1923, netted Anna $2,500 on a policy written up less than a year before. But apparently, that windfall was insufficient to cover Anna's pecuniary needs. That same year, two more of her children, Charles, 18, and 13-year-old Walter, died. Their deaths brought $850 and $180 respectively.

Now only David Jr. and Mae survived, and it looked like David was soon to join his brethren in the ground. He was seized suddenly by violent attacks and lay writhing and thrashing on the bed in agony. Fortunately for David (and unfortunately for his mother), Mae insisted that he be taken to hospital. Anna could hardly refuse when her son was in such obvious agony and an ambulance was called.

Dr. Thomas Carver examined David on admission and immediately recognized his symptoms. An antidote was given and although he remained paralyzed for several weeks after, David eventually made a full recovery. Tests proved that he'd ingested copious amounts of arsenic.

Now suddenly, the curse of the Cunninghams was explained. Exhumations were ordered and proved that each of the family had been poisoned. When a large quantity of the poison was found in the Cunningham household, Anna Cunningham was arrested.

Initially, she insisted that the poison was an insecticide that she sprayed on her plants. When detectives pressed her on the issue, she feigned a fit and lapsed into a "coma."

Revived after several hours, she eventually broke down and confessed to killing her children. She'd fed them the arsenic on bread and butter sandwiches she said. However, money wasn't the motive she insisted. She only wanted to reunite the children with their father in heaven.

Anna Cunningham was tried and convicted of killing her youngest son, Walter. She was sentenced to life in prison and spent the rest of her days behind bars.

Robert Danielson

In the summer of 1982, Robert Danielson and his girlfriend, Lanora Johnson, hitchhiked from Oregon to California. Danielson had recently been released from a prison term for a 1970 homicide, and the trip was in contravention of his parole conditions. That didn't bother him much. In the year since his release, he'd already committed enough crimes to put him back in prison for good.

In July 1982, Danielson and Johnson showed up at a trailer park in Mendocino County, California. Short of funds, they decided to rob someone and chose as their victims, Benjamin and Edith Shaffer, a couple both in their sixties. Danielson knocked on the door of the Shaffer's camper and, when it was opened, forced the elderly couple inside at gunpoint. He then tied his victims up and instructed Johnson to take their dog for a walk.

Johnson had covered only a short distance when she heard gunshots. When she returned to the camper, she found that both Mr. and Mrs. Shaffer had been shot in the head. Danielson told her to help him dispose of the bodies, which they did by rolling them down an embankment. Danielson then ransacked the camper, stealing traveler's checks, credit cards, and other possessions. The Shaffers' bodies would lay undiscovered for two years.

The murder of the elderly couple was by no means the first committed by Danielson since his release from prison. On December 10, 1981, 60-year-old Harold Pratt and his wife Betty, 55, were camping in the Arizona desert, some 75 miles southeast of Phoenix, when they were surprised and overpowered. The Tucson residents were robbed of their possessions then shot execution-style in the back of the head, their bodies left to the coyotes.

On June 25, 1982, 62-year-old Arthur Gray Jr. was robbed and killed in similar fashion at the Twin Springs Campground, 80 miles to the east of Eugene, Oregon. Danielson then headed for California, where he murdered Benjamin and Edith Shaffer, before returning to Arizona.

With the money he'd stolen from the Shaffers running low, he struck again in November 1982. The victim was 38-year-old Ernest Corral, shot in the head, his body dumped in a ravine near his hometown of Apache Junction, Arizona.

The police were by this time hunting Danielson on a number of charges, including check fraud, driving with a suspended license and parole violations. Most serious of all was the attempted murder of an elderly couple in El Cajon, California, on March 22, 1982. Edwin and Ida Davis, both 64, had befriended a younger couple and welcomed them into their home. Their new acquaintances reciprocated their kindness by overpowering them and injecting them with large doses of a powerful horse tranquilizer, enough to kill.

Left for dead, Edwin and Ida were found by friends who rushed them to hospital. They were later able to identify Robert Danielson from mugshots.

On February 9, 1984, a federal warrant was issued for Danielson's arrest and on April 7, FBI agents tracked him to Odessa, Texas, where he was working with a traveling carnival. The seven-time killer surrendered without a fight.

Danielson was returned to Oregon to face trial, earning a life sentence there in 1985. In 1986, he was extradited to California, where the testimony of his former girlfriend secured a guilty verdict for the murders of Benjamin and Edith Shaffer. Danielson was sentenced to death on November 13, 1986.

Bruce Davis

Bruce Davis carried a festering anger with him, a toxic hatred of homosexuals resulting from a sexual assault he'd endured at age 13.

Born in 1948, in Toledo, Ohio, Davis was raised in rural Fayette County. As a child he was often complimented on his singing talent, so much so that he began to believe that a career in show business awaited him. To this extent, he dropped out of school in the mid-sixties and hopped a Greyhound bus to New York City.

Davis took menial jobs in New York while he completed his high school diploma at night school and shopped his talent around as a singer. However, like so many young hopefuls before him, he found the entertainment industry a hard nut to crack. Eventually, worn down by the rejections, fed up at working long hours for minimum wage, frustrated by his lack of progress, he hatched a new plan.

There were lots of wealthy gay men in the city willing to pay for the companionship of a handsome, young man. They were easy to lure, easy to overpower and rob. The added bonus was that he'd be hitting back at homosexuals, who he by now blamed for everything that had gone wrong in his life.

Over the next four years, Davis traveled the country, carrying out his plan. His M.O. was simplicity itself. He'd cruise gay bars and bathhouses, hone in on a victim he figured was well off, then convince the man into taking him home for sex. Once there, Davis would overpower, beat and rob his victim. Sometimes he'd go further, torturing and killing the man.

The law eventually caught up with Davis in February 1972, when he was arrested in Washington D.C. for the murder of local businessman, James Earl Hammer. Convicted of manslaughter, he was sentenced to five to fifteen years in prison. Then Illinois authorities linked him with the strangulation death of Reverend Carlo Barlassina, killed in a Chicago hotel on June 29, 1971.

Davis was extradited to Illinois to face charges in the Barlassina killing. He was convicted of murder in December 1972, drawing a 25-to-45-year prison term to run consecutively with his current sentence. That sentence was completed eight and a half years later and Davis was then moved from the federal lockup at Terre Haute, Indiana, to the Illinois state prison at Menard.

On the afternoon of October 24, 1982, while on a work detail outside the prison gates, Davis attacked prison guard Joe Cushman with an ax, killing him. He then fled in Cushman's car, abandoning the vehicle the following day, near Christopher, Illinois. He remained at large until October 31, when officers in Smithers, West Virginia, arrested him as he tried to steal a car.

Returned to custody in Illinois, a despondent Davis gave prison authorities a rambling confession, claiming 32 murders between

1969 and 1971. He'd killed at least eight victims in Washington D.C. he said, five in New York, with others in Baltimore, Boston, Fort Lauderdale, Reno, Las Vegas, New Orleans, Los Angeles, and San Juan, Puerto Rico. Without exception, the victims were wealthy, homosexual men.

Many of the murders checked out, and although Davis was able to provide details only the killer would know, he'd never stand trial for those killings. He would, however, be tried for the murder of Joe Cushman, a crime that earned him a life sentence without parole.

David Dowler

One thing common to most serial killers is the rich fantasy lives they live. Often these involve torture and mutilation, aberrant sex and revenge for perceived slights. David Dowler's fantasies, though, read like something straight out of James Bond.

A native of Albuquerque, New Mexico, Dowler was the son of an Air Force colonel and his Japanese wife. He seemed a well-adjusted child, did reasonably well at school and was on the wrestling team. In his spare time, he dabbled in electronics and operated a ham radio. After high school, he spent three years in college before dropping out. Along the way, he earned himself a black belt in karate.

In 1981, Dowler moved to Odessa, Texas, where he found employment as a sales representative for an oil company. Dowler was good at his job and popular with his co-workers, even if they considered him a bit of an oddball. To those in his inner circle, he was fond of telling tales about working undercover for the government and having assassinated six enemy agents. Most of them took these stories with a pinch of salt. Soon they'd have call to reassess their skepticism.

On the morning of August 16, 1983, Dowler phoned the father of one of his co-workers, 26-year-old Lisa Krieg. Lisa was late for work, he said, and he was worried about her.

Somewhat perplexed by the call, Lisa's father decided to check on her anyway. He found his daughter's partially clad body stretched out across her bed.

Lisa's death was put down to a longstanding battle with anorexia. No one thought to ask Dowler how'd he'd known she'd be dead, but he told them anyway. Lisa had been a spy, he said, and he knew through his contacts that enemy agents had tried to kill her several times before. He also said that it was he who had discovered the body. He'd found her nude and had "put some clothes on her," before calling her father.

Dowler had his next deadly premonition two and a half years later, on February 12, 1986. Juan Casillas was Dowler's partner in a one-hour photo developing service. On the day in question, Dowler called Casillas's ex-wife, Leza Chandler, to say that he was "worried about Juan." Taking the warning to heart, Chandler stopped at her ex-husband's home and found him dead on the kitchen floor. Traces of drugs were found in his system, but the cause of death was recorded as "unknown."

Dowler's next premonition involved Leza Chandler herself. On June 28, 1987, he phoned one of Chandler's friends and advised her to check on Leza, "just in case." The friend found Leza's body in her bed, her infant daughter lying beside her.

This time, the cause of death was more clear-cut. Leza Chandler had died of chloroform poisoning, leading to suspicion falling on Dowler. He was placed under surveillance and a lady friend agreed to wear a wire while carrying on a conversation with him. Although Dowler said nothing directly incriminating, he spoke at length about spies, assassinations, and how to kill someone with chloroform.

Dowler was arrested on August 20, 1987. A search of his apartment netted bottles of chloroform, a .22-caliber pistol, and two homemade silencers.

Meanwhile, forensic tests on Lisa Krieg and Juan Casillas turned up lethal levels of cyanide. Police also looked into another death among Dowler's close acquaintances. Dorothy Nesbitt had died under mysterious circumstances in November 1986. No charges would be filed in this case.

On January 27, 1988, Dowler was convicted of first-degree murder and sentenced to life in prison.

No motive has ever been offered for the murders he committed. The trial judge probably came close when he noted in his summation that Dowler enjoyed having the power to "snuff out somebody's life."

Jeffrey Lynn Feltner

Jeffrey Lynn Feltner was born in Miami, Florida. He was raised in a single parent home, his father having abandoned the family three months before Jeff's birth. The youngest of four children, Jeff grew up to be a timid boy, who endured constant teasing because of his diminutive size. Even as an adult, he stood only five-foot-three and weighed just over 100 pounds.

When Feltner was 16, his mother remarried and the family moved to Melrose, Florida. Feltner seemed to adjust well to his new surroundings and did reasonably well at school. Unbeknownst to his mother, he was also pursuing clandestine activities. It was in Melrose that he first started visiting gay hangouts.

While still in high school, Feltner had begun helping out at the hospital where his mother worked as a nurse. After graduating, he found employment there as a nurse's aide, working the 3 p.m. to 11 p.m. shift. He showed a real aptitude for the work and within a short time had been promoted to aide supervisor.

In July 1988, an anonymous caller phoned a local television station. Claiming to be a nurse's aide, the caller confessed to killing several patients at the nursing home where he worked. The caller said that the murders had been mercy killings and that there were three female and two male victims. He also warned that he would likely kill again.

The information was passed on to the police, who investigated the caller's claims. However, they could find no evidence of murder. Nonetheless, the investigation did reveal the source of the anonymous calls. Jeffrey Feltner was arrested and charged with making harassing phone calls, trespass, and filing a false report. He was found guilty on all charges and spent four months in jail.

After his release, Feltner visited his father in Michigan and then moved back to Florida where he found an apartment in Daytona Beach. He signed on at a temporary agency for healthcare professionals and was soon working again, gaining positions at a number of nursing homes including Clyatt Memorial Center and facilities in Ormond Beach and Putnam County. At around this time, Feltner was diagnosed with AIDS.

In August 1989, he began making anonymous phone calls again, this time using the alias "Jack." On August 3, he phoned TV station WESH in Daytona Beach and said that he had a friend who was killing patients at a nursing home. He called again on August 9, and made the same allegation, this time adding that the patients had been suffocated to "ease their pain." The station passed on the information to the police, but it was only when Feltner confessed to his roommate that he was eventually arrested.

Under interrogation, Feltner openly admitted to seven murders. However, as most of the alleged victims had been cremated, the police were unable to corroborate his confessions to five of the murders. In the other two, there were clear signs that the victims had died as Feltner said, by suffocation.

Feltner was charged with two murders. But before the matter came to trial, he recanted his confessions. He now claimed that it had all been a ploy, to draw attention to the poor conditions in nursing homes. It was too late now. The police had definite evidence of foul play, evidence that would have passed unnoticed had Feltner kept his mouth shut.

Feltner was eventually found guilty on one charge of first-degree murder and one charge of second-degree murder. He was sentenced to life in prison, with a mandatory 25-year minimum. He would serve only two years before dying of AIDS on March 17, 1993.

Charles Floyd

On July 10, 1942, William Brown, a trucker from Tulsa, Oklahoma, returned home to discover his heavily pregnant wife lying dead on the floor. He immediately called the police who determined that 20-year-old Mary Brown, just 6 days from the delivery of her child, had been raped and strangled. The apartment was left in disarray but none of the neighbors had seen or heard anything unusual. Neither were there any clues left at the scene. Before long, the leads had dried up and the case went cold.

Six months later, in January 1943, Clara Stewart and her married daughter, Georgina Green, were beaten to death in an apartment close to where Mary Brown had been killed. Georgina had been living with her mother while her husband was serving in the army. A subsequent autopsy indicated that the women had been raped after death.

There was another peculiarity. Both women had naturally red hair, a trait shared by previous victim, Mary Brown. Given the close proximity of the two murder scenes the police believed that a single perpetrator was responsible, a killer who targeted redheads.

This theory was given credence on May 15, 1945, when another redhead, Panta Lou Niles, was bludgeoned to death as she slept. The killer had entered through an open window and remained in the room for several hours, committing necrophilia on the corpse. When a friend phoned Ms. Niles early the next morning to wake her for work, she was startled to hear a man's voice on the other end of the line. She hung up immediately and phoned the police. By the time they arrived the killer had fled.

The latest murder caused an uproar, placing the Tulsa Police Department under immense pressure to catch the killer. They responded by arresting a known sex offender, a slow-witted drifter named Henry Owens. Owens agreed to take a polygraph but the results were inconclusive.

At any rate, Owens was soon off the hook. He was still in custody on July 1, 1948, when the killer struck again, carrying out four attacks in a single night.

First, he broke into an apartment and assaulted the female occupant, her 12-year-old daughter, and a young friend who was sleeping over. After bludgeoning the three victims, he undressed them, then began raping the woman. Fortunately, one of the girls regained consciousness and started screaming, attracting the attention of the neighbor and causing the assailant to flee. He was not to be denied, though. Just a couple of blocks away, he broke into the home of Ruth Norton – another redhead – beating her to death before raping her corpse.

The killer had now claimed five lives, but this latest murder had at last provided investigators with a description, the witness adding the odd detail that the man he saw leaving the Norton residence "looked like a truck driver."

Odd or not, the police were by now desperate to make an arrest and followed up on the clue. Canvassing the local trucking companies, they soon got to hear about Charles Floyd, a driver who talked obsessively about redheads, and who had quit his job and skipped town on the morning of July 2, directly after the Norton murder. Floyd was eventually tracked to Dallas and arrested on November 22, 1949.

Floyd initially denied involvement in the murders, but quickly implicated himself with his convoluted alibis and his knowledge of the crime scenes. Eventually, he broke down and confessed, claiming that he'd begun by peeping at Panta Niles as she undressed in front of an open window. Unable to control the lust that his voyeuristic activities triggered, he had devolved to rape and murder.

Charles Floyd would never be tried for the murders he committed. Judged insane, he was confined to an asylum in 1949. He remained there for the rest of his life.

Lester Harrison

Between 1970 and 1973, a grisly series of murders occurred in and around Grant Park in downtown Chicago. The victims were bludgeoned, stabbed, or throttled to death. Some were mutilated after death. In at least one instance there was evidence that the killer had gnawed on the corpse.

The first to die was Agnes Lehman, beaten to death near the park's bandstand on July 10, 1970, her body discovered the next morning. A shoe found at the scene was linked to a man named Wilbur McDonald, who was arrested 12 days later.

McDonald admitted to being with Lehman on the night of her death but claimed that, as they stood near the bandstand, a black man had suddenly charged out of the dark and attacked them. McDonald had fled, losing a shoe in the process.

The story sounded far-fetched and the jury wasn't buying it. McDonald was found guilty of murder and sentenced to 150 years in prison. He had already begun his prison term when another woman, Judith Betteley, was attacked and beaten to death near the Grant Park bandstand on September 5, 1972.

Three weeks later, Chicago police arrested Lester Harrison on a charge of assaulting a 31-year-old woman with a brick. Released on bond of $5,000, Harrison was found competent to stand trial and was formally indicted on December 29. In the meanwhile, he remained on bail.

In July 1973, Irene Koutros was stabbed to death in Grant Park's underground garage. Three weeks later, on August 3, Lee Wilson was fatally stabbed in the park. When her body was discovered, it bore clear indications that the assailant had tried to rip away chunks of flesh with his teeth.

Ten days after the Wilson murder, 28-year-old Judith Ott was knifed to death in a Grant Park restroom. Her husband, waiting for her outside, saw a black man sprint from the scene of the attack. Still unaware that his wife had been killed, David Ott gave chase and tackled Harrison, then held him until the police arrived.

Under interrogation, Harrison confessed to four of the Grant Park murders, although he denied killing Irene Koutros. Harrison was forthright when asked about his motive for the murders. The thought of female suffering aroused him, he said, and he derived great satisfaction from beating and stabbing his victims.

Harrison was indicted on four murders, but before he could stand trial there was the issue of competence. Over the years, Harrison had spent numerous periods of incarceration in state hospitals. In addition, he'd previously been ruled incompetent to stand trial in another murder, that of fellow inmate Norman Kimme, in 1951.

In this case, he was ruled competent, although the eventual outcome of the trial was a disappointment to prosecutors. Harrison was found not guilty by reason of insanity.

However, the idea of setting a schizophrenic sex killer free, appalled state prosecutors and they, therefore, convened a special hearing to have Harrison declared "sexually dangerous," under a seldom-used state statute. As a result of the hearing, Harrison was declared a menace to society and ordered confined indefinitely.

In May 1986, Harrison's attorneys made a bid to free their client. By now, the 62-year-old was a quadriplegic who his defense team described as "harmless." Staff at Belleville State Hospital told a different story. They related how Harrison could still move his arms, and how he became physically aroused in the presence of female staff. The petition was denied.

James R. Hicks

Twenty-two-year-old Jennie Lynn Hicks had gone missing from her home in Carmel, Maine on July 19, 1977. Her husband, James, said he had no knowledge of her whereabouts. The police thought he was lying but with no evidence to prove their suspicions they were forced to let the matter lie.

Five years passed. Then in October 1982, James Hicks' name popped up in connection with the disappearance of another woman. Jerilyn Towers, 34, had vanished after leaving a bar in the company of Hicks on October 16. Hicks again pled innocence. Again there was insufficient evidence to charge him. However, in a bizarre twist, investigators looking into the Jerilyn Towers case turned up evidence that implicated Hicks in the 1977 disappearance of his wife. Charged with murder, Hicks was sentenced to 10 years in prison. He was paroled in 1990.

After his release from prison, Hicks found work at the Twin City Motel in Brewer, Maine. There, he became involved in a relationship with a co-worker, Lynn Willette.

Hicks and Willette moved in together at an apartment on South Main Street. But in May 1996, Willette disappeared, with Hicks declaring that he had no idea where she was. Without evidence of wrongdoing, the police were again forced to let him walk, even though they were sure by now that they were dealing with a serial killer.

Hicks next showed up in Lubbock, Texas, having moved there from Maine in 1999. On April 8, 2000, he held a 67-year-old woman at gunpoint, forcing her to write him a check for $1,250, and to sign over the title to her car. He then made her write a suicide note before forcing her to drink cough syrup.

Hick's plan was to make the victim drowsy before drowning her in the bathtub, making it look like a suicide. Unfortunately for him, the woman escaped and later testified at his trial. Hicks was convicted on a charge of aggravated robbery and sentenced to 55 years in prison.

The prospect of a long term in a Texas prison apparently held little appeal for James Hicks. He'd barely begun his sentence when he sent out an S.O.S to the authorities in Maine, offering to cop to two murder charges as well as pointing out the location of three missing women. All he wanted in exchange was to serve his time in Maine rather than Texas.

The chance to close two unsolved homicides and to bring closure to three families was too good for the Maine authorities to turn down. A deal was duly struck with Texas and Hicks was returned to his home state.

In terms of the agreement, Hicks then made a full confession to the murders of Jerilyn Towers and Lynn Willette. He also led investigators to the bodies of his three victims. Towers and his former wife, Jennie Lynn, were buried just 100 feet apart, near his former home in Etna. Willette's remains were found encased in concrete filled buckets, buried next to a road in Aroostook County. All three corpses had been dismembered, with some parts allegedly tossed into a nearby river.

Hicks received life sentences for each of the murders. Should he ever be paroled in Maine he will be required to serve out the remainder of his sentence in Texas.

Clarence Hill

On the crisp Saturday evening of September 30, 1939, Frank Kasper, 28, and Katherine Werner, 36, drove to a desolate stretch of road on Duck Island, near Trenton, New Jersey. The two had good reason for being out here at night, they were both married and involved in an illicit affair. Stopping under the cover of some trees, they began kissing and fondling each other. Neither noticed the man who stepped from the undergrowth carrying a shotgun.

The man was standing beside the car when he fired, striking Frank Kasper in the head and neck, killing him instantly. Katherine Werner jumped from the vehicle and ran, but she'd made it only a few feet before the assassin fired again. The first shot tore off her lower right arm. The second pulverized her head.

The police were called to the crime scene the following morning. This was the second double homicide that had occurred at Duck Island in the past year and investigators knew now that they were hunting a serial killer, someone the media dubbed the "Duck Island Killer."

The first murder had occurred on November 8, 1938. Vincent Tonzillo and Mary Myatovich had driven out to Duck Island to spend some time together. Like, Kasper and Werner, they had good reason to keep their affair secret. Twenty-year-old Tonzillo was married, and Mary Myatovich's father had forbidden him from seeing the 15-year-old Mary.

The couple arrived at the lover's lane at around 7 p.m. It was raining outside, making visibility difficult, so they were caught completely by surprise when a man suddenly threw the door open.

"This is a stickup," he said.

Before either could reply the gunman fired, killing Tonzillo. Myatovich was hauled from the car but managed to wriggle free and run, making a few steps before the attacker shot her in the buttocks. Then he raped her before leaving her for dead in the road. Another driver found her there at 8:30 p.m.

Mary survived for another 36 hours at St. Francis Hospital. Before she died she identified her attacker as a black man but was unable to provide any details that might help police catch the killer. Investigators were skeptical of the description anyway. They believed a jealous lover or angry relative was responsible. Only after the Kaspar / Werner double murder did they realize what they were dealing with.

With police attention now focused on Duck Island, the killer struck next outside Morrisville, Pennsylvania, on November 2, 1940. The victims survived, although the man was injured. Two weeks later, he was back at his favorite hunting ground. Louis Kovacs, 25, and Carolina Morconi, 27, were shot at such close range that there were powder burns on their faces.

The case had, by now, attracted national attention, with American Weekly declaring in an article that the killer would definitely strike again in 1941. He didn't, waiting instead until April 7, 1942.

This time, the couple survived, albeit with horrendous injuries. John Testa, a newly enlisted soldier, lost an arm. His girlfriend, Antoinette Marcantonio, was viciously beaten with the gunstock.

But the killer had made a mistake. When he'd clubbed Marcantonio, the wooden stock of the 20-gauge shotgun had come off. Etched into the wood was the serial number "A-639," and although it took more than a year of painstaking investigative work, the weapon was eventually traced to a Hamilton resident named Clarence Hill.

Hill was a 34-year-old married man, who worked as a laborer and taught Sunday school at the Mount Olivet Baptist Church. He was also a sexual pervert who had carried on affairs with a number of his teenaged students and had impregnated one of them.

Arrested in December 1943, Hill confessed to the murders, claiming he'd committed them in order to have sex with the female victims. He was sentenced to life imprisonment but served fewer than 20 years before being paroled in 1964. He died of natural causes on July 9, 1973.

Johnny Ray Johnson

A horrendously brutal rape slayer, Johnny Ray Johnson would eventually be executed for the 1995 murder of Leah Joette Smith. But as savage as that crime was, it was only the tip of a decades-long campaign of sexual violence against women perpetrated by the Austin, Texas, taxi driver.

According to Johnson's confession, he met Leah Smith on March 27, 1995. Johnson offered Smith some crack cocaine in exchange for sex, to which she readily agreed. However, after smoking the crack, she reneged and refused to sleep with him. Angered by her refusal, Johnson grabbed her, ripped her clothing and threw her to the ground. When she fought back he struck her head repeatedly against the cement curb. He then raped her, after which he stomped on her face five or six times and left her for dead.

Later, he realized that he'd dropped his wallet at the scene and returned to retrieve it. Finding Smith dead, he had sex with her corpse before leaving. An autopsy would later determine that she'd suffered severe injuries to her mouth, face, head, and neck. Her teeth were knocked out, and both sides of her jaw were fractured. Death, though, was due to drowning on her own blood as it accumulated in the back of her throat.

Eventually arrested for the murder, Johnson went on trial in May 1996, where the prosecution introduced evidence documenting his horrific criminal past, stretching back to 1975. In that year, Johnson raped his eight-year-old niece, threatening to kill the child if she told anyone.

In 1983, he was convicted of sexual assault in Travis County and was sentenced to five years in prison. Upon his release, he found employment driving cabs in Houston. One of his favorite ruses during this period, was to pick up prostitutes, drive them out to the country, then rape them before driving off with their money and clothes. He also preyed on his ordinary customers, on one occasion beating and raping a woman after she refused his offer of $20 in exchange for sex. The woman was able to identify him, resulting in a five-year prison term.

In 1991, Johnson married prostitute Dora Ann Moseley and moved to Austin. The marriage ended in 1994 after Johnson beat his wife so badly that she would probably have died had a neighbor not called the police. That vicious assault earned Johnson a meager six months in prison.

Released in the summer of 1994, Johnson soon graduated to murder. According to his confession, his first victim was a woman he met on 11th Street in Austin. The two spent some time together, drinking and smoking crack. But when he tried to have sex with the woman, she refused, producing a razor and slashing his neck. Johnson fought back, beating his companion into submission before raping her. Afterwards, he used the woman's razor to cut off her head, which he carried from the scene and later used for "irregular sex."

Johnson committed several more rapes in Austin before returning to Houston in December 1994. In February 1995, he raped his brother's common-law wife, an offense that went unreported until his confession.

On March 27, 1995, the badly decomposed body of a woman was found in a water-filled gully near some railroad tracks. The victim had sustained severe head injuries and had also been strangled. The crime remained unsolved until Johnson confessed to raping the woman and beating her to death with a rock. He claimed another victim in similar fashion just three days later.

On April 28, 1995, the partially clothed body of a woman was found under a highway overpass in Houston. She had sustained massive head injuries, while markings on her throat suggested that her killer had stomped on her. Johnson confessed to the murder, admitting that he'd bludgeoned the woman with a block of concrete (A bloodstained breezeblock had, in fact, been found at the scene).

Johnson's trial concluded in May 1996, with a guilty verdict and death penalty. He was executed by lethal injection on February 12, 2009.

Anthony Joyner

The Kearsley Home, at Christ Church Hospital in Philadelphia, Pennsylvania, is the oldest nursing home in the United States. This specialist facility caters to the elderly and infirm, providing an environment where they can spend their final years under the caring attention of professional staff. It is hardly the kind of place where you'd expect to find a serial killer at work.

And yet, between January and July 1983, just such a creature was active at the Kearsley. This vile fiend preyed on the weakest of the weak, raping and killing frail six women, their ages ranging from 80 to 92 years.

Given the age of the average patient at the home, death is not altogether unexpected and the first two murders slipped by undetected, the victims thought to have died as the result of cardiac arrest. But something about the death of the third victim, 86-year-old, Kathryn Maxwell, did not seem right to staff at the clinic. Ms. Maxwell had died during a blizzard on February 12, 1983, her body found in her room the following morning. Her death, like the others, was put down to a heart attack.

Despite the staff's suspicions, there was nothing to indicate foul play and, as Ms. Maxwell's body had been donated to medical science, it was transferred to the University of Pennsylvania medical school, for use in anatomy classes.

Over the next two months, two more elderly patients - Eugenia Border, 90, and Mildred Alston, 83, died at the home under circumstances very similar to Kathryn Maxwell. With suspicions now roused, an autopsy was ordered on Ms. Maxwell, her cadaver still in storage at the university hospital. The examination was carried out by assistant medical examiner, Dr. Herbert Fillinger, and revealed that the elderly victim had been suffocated.

As detectives began questioning staff at the clinic, suspicion fell on one man, Anthony Joyner, a 24-year-old who worked in the kitchen. Joyner was initially arrested on two counts of murder, with a further four charges later added to the docket. He went on trial in May 1984 and was found guilty on all six counts.

Given the heinous nature of the crimes, the prosecution had argued hard for the death penalty. However, in order for that sentence to be passed, the jury had to be unanimous in their decision during the penalty phase. In this case, they weren't, allowing one of the most depraved killers in Pennsylvania history to escape with his life.

Anthony Joyner was sentenced to life in prison on May 5, 1984. It is highly unlikely that he will ever be released.

Steven Judy

A minority of serial killers emerge from backgrounds that are seemingly normal. There was little indication in the childhoods of Ted Bundy and Jeffrey Dahmer, for example, to suggest the monsters they would become.

In other cases, there is no doubt whatsoever. Steven Timothy Judy was just 12 years old when, on a summer day in 1968, he knocked on the door of a young housewife in the neighborhood where he lived. He was dressed in a Boy Scout uniform and claimed to be selling cookies. However, when the woman turned her back on him to fetch her purse, he suddenly attacked her, plunging a pocket knife repeatedly into her back with such violence that the blade eventually broke. He then dragged the stricken woman to the bedroom where he raped her, before attempting to kill her with a hatchet. One of the victim's fingers was severed as she raised her hand to protect herself, but despite Judy's efforts, she survived and was able to name him as her assailant. The attack earned the juvenile offender just nine months of treatment in a mental institution.

The therapy proved ineffective. At age 18, Judy was convicted of aggravated assault on a woman in Chicago, earning a 20-month stretch. No sooner had he been released than he was in trouble again, this time for abducting a female motorist and forcing her to drive out into the country. Fortunately, the woman escaped and was able to identify Judy as her abductor. He earned a year in jail for kidnapping. He was out by 1977.

On April 28, 1979, mushroom hunters walking along White Lick Creek, just outside of Indianapolis, were shocked to discover the naked corpse of a woman. They immediately ran to call the police, who were soon on the scene.

Worse was to follow. Further downstream, tangled in some branches were the corpses of three small children – two boys and a girl. It appeared that the woman had been raped and strangled, the children had then fallen (or been thrown) into the stream and had drowned.

A driver's license found nearby identified the adult victim as 23-year-old Terry Chasteen. Following up on this lead, police learned that Chasteen, a divorcee, had left her home at around 7 a.m. to drop her children off at a babysitter before going to her job at a Marsh's department store. Neither Chasteen nor her children had made it to their destination.

As the police put out a public appeal for information, details emerged of a distinctive red-and-silver pickup truck, seen near the murder scene. It was traced eventually to 22-year-old Steven Judy, a construction worker.

Judy was arrested at the home of his foster parents and wasted no time in confessing to the murders. He said that he'd been driving alongside Terry Chasteen when he'd decided he wanted to rape her. Drawing her attention, he'd indicated that there was something wrong with the rear wheel of her car. After Chasteen pulled over, Judy stopped beside her and offered to help. He pretended to fasten the wheel lugs and then offered to look under the hood when Chasteen had difficulty starting the car. Instead of fixing the vehicle, he disabled it.

Continuing in his role as the "knight in shining armor" Judy then offered to drive Chasteen and her children to where they needed to be. Instead, he took them to White Lick Creek, walked them into the woods, and told the children to go and play down by the water. He then began raping Chasteen, but her cries brought the children running back, so Judy strangled her. In an act of inhuman depravity, he then threw 5-year-old Misty, 4-year-old Mark, and 2-year-old Steven into the creek, leaving them to drown.

Judy went on trial for the murders in early 1980. Found guilty, he was given the opportunity to address the jury before sentencing. "You'd better put me to death," he sneered, "because next time it might be one of you or your daughters."

Shaken by this outburst the 9-man, 3 women, jury was happy to oblige, recommending that Judy be put to death in the electric chair.

Immediately after sentencing, Judy instructed his lawyers not to file any appeals on his behalf. He spent his time on death row admitting to a series of other murders, spanning Indiana, Illinois, Louisiana, Texas, and Florida. At least four of his confessions checked out.

Steven Judy was executed in Indiana's electric chair on March 8, 1981.

James Koedatich

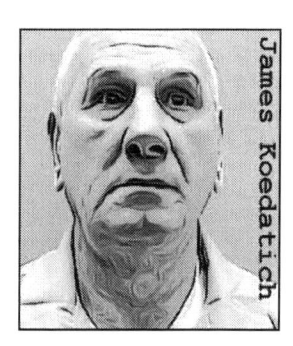

In August 1982, James Koedatich walked free from Raiford prison in Florida, having served 11 years for the strangulation murder of his roommate, Robert Anderson, in June 1971. That Koedatich was considered for early release was something of a surprise, given that he'd strangled another man to death while serving his prison term. However, in that case, the prison authorities had accepted Koedatich's version of events and ruled the homicide self-defense.

Gaining permission from Florida state officials, Koedatich moved north, settling in Morristown, New Jersey, in September 1982. Barely two months later, on November 23, 1982, 18-year-old Amie Hoffman, a Parsippany Hills High School cheerleader, went missing from the parking lot of a Morris County shopping mall. Amy's body was found two days later, on Thanksgiving Day. She'd been raped and stabbed to death with a long-bladed hunting knife, her corpse dumped in a retention basin at the Mendham Reservoir in Randolph Township.

Responding to police requests for information, several witnesses came forward to describe a man seen with Amy both at the mall and on a bridge near the reservoir. However, the descriptions were conflicting and police were no closer to resolving the case 12 days later, when another woman was murdered.

Twenty-nine-year-old Deirdre O'Brian was pulled from her car at a Route 80 rest area near Allamuchy, 20 miles from Morristown. She was raped and stabbed in the chest, her attacker then fleeing the scene, leaving her for dead. Deirdre was found shortly after by another motorist. She lived just long enough to provide a description of her attacker. He looked "like a truck driver," she said.

It didn't leave the police much to go on, and the killer would likely have remained at large to kill again. However, like many serial killers before him, James Koedatich foolishly decided to insert himself into the investigation.

On the night of January 16, 1983, he placed a call to Morristown police and reported that he'd been attacked and stabbed in the back after stopping beside a road in Morris County, just a quarter-mile from the scene of the O'Brian murder.

The authorities initially believed that the attacker might have been the same man who was responsible for O'Brian's death. But as they looked into Koedatich's story, they began to suspect that he was lying. Then, a check on the tires of Koedatich's vehicle provided a match to tracks found at the second murder scene, and Koedatich found himself under arrest.

Held in lieu of $250,000 bail, he was formally charged with Deirdre O'Brian's murder on May 12. On December 15, a second indictment was added, for murdering Amy Hoffman.

Koedatich stood trial for the Hoffman murder first and in October 1984 he was found guilty of murder, kidnapping, aggravated sexual assault, and unlawful possession of a weapon with intent to kill. On October 29, Koedatich became the first man sentenced to death under New Jersey's revised capital punishment statute (the sentence was later commuted to life imprisonment).

Another conviction followed in May 1985, for the murder of Deirdre O'Brian. In this case, the jury balked at sending him to the chair, voting for life imprisonment instead.

William Darrell Lindsey

"You've got to understand that there's a good Bill and a bad Bill. Good Bill is a decent person. Bad Bill is a person society needs to be afraid of."

Those were the words of serial killer William Lindsey, shortly after his arrest in Asherville, North Carolina, on December 29, 1996. North Carolina authorities did not realize it yet, but they'd just captured the man who had terrorized St. Augustine, Florida, for over a decade, committing at least seven homicides, and possibly as many as 23.

Born in St. Augustine on March 18, 1935, Lindsey was orphaned in infancy and adopted soon after. His adoptive mother proved to be a sadistic woman who subjected the young boy to horrific physical and psychological abuse. As a child, Lindsey displayed many of the classic signs of an emerging serial killer – animal torture, fire starting, emotional detachment, and violent outbursts. As he grew older he became a heavy drinker and drug user. He also developed a weirdly warped sexuality - he was impotent unless enraged.

On the evening of October 9, 1983, prostitute Lisa Foley left the Tradewinds Lounge in downtown St. Augustine in the company of a man and promptly disappeared. Five days later, her body was discovered in a marshy area near St. Augustine Beach. Her murder would remain unsolved until Lindsey confessed in 1997.

Anita McQuaig got into Lindsey's car in downtown St. Augustine at around 7 p.m. on November 29, 1988. Her body was discovered the following morning. She had been beaten so badly that her eye socket had collapsed and her jaw was fractured in multiple places. Her nude body also bore signs of torture, including cigarette burns and bite marks.

Another streetwalker, Connie Terrell, was picked up by Lindsey at "Crackhead Corner," a local pickup spot, on the evening of Saturday, June 10, 1989. Twelve hours later, her nude body was found half-submerged in a pond off Holmes Boulevard. She had been strangled with a rope and shot in the head with a .22-caliber pistol.

Lashawna Streeter also disappeared from Crackhead Corner after accepting a "date" with Lindsey on March 1, 1992. Ten days later her severely battered body was found in a field near State Road 207. She'd been kicked and beaten to death.

The next to die was Cheryl Lucas. Picked up by Lindsey on a rainy summer night in June 1995, she was found beaten to death several days later. According to Lindsey's later confession, Lucas had snatched some money he had lying on the dashboard and made a run for it. He'd caught up with her near some railroad tracks and beaten her to death with a crowbar.

Lindsey also confessed to the murders of Donetha Haile and Diana Richardson, although their bodies have never been found.

Given the profile of the victims – drug addicted prostitutes – the murders aroused very little public outcry in St. Augustine. But at least one law officer remained determined to solve them. Deputy Fred Thompson had already retired from the force when he sent his former boss, Sheriff Neil Perry, a Christmas card in December 1996. Enclosed with the card was a newspaper clipping about the Anita McQuaig murder, a not too subtle reminder that a serial killer was still loose on the streets of St. Augustine.

Thompson forwarded the clipping to St. Johns' County cold case detectives in January 1997. Their subsequent investigation led them to William Lindsey, currently serving time for murder in North Carolina.

Lindsey was extradited to Florida in July 1999, and pled guilty to six counts of murder in order to avoid the death penalty. He is due to be released on December 11, 2025, by which time he will be 90 years of age.

Dorothy Matajke

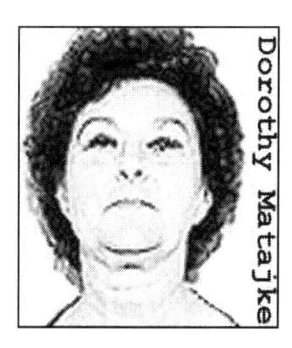

Among the most heinous of killers are caregivers who murder their patients. These callous reprobates most often target children and the elderly, and their method of murder, usually poison, inflicts a painful and lingering death on those who rely on them for their health and wellbeing.

One such person was Dorothy Matajke. A native of Iowa, Matajke began working as a companion to the elderly in the 1970s. It is a profession that is much in demand, which perhaps explains why Matajke was seldom out of work, even though her elderly charges seemed to have a limited lifespan under her care. When she did eventually attract the attention of the authorities, it was not for these mysterious deaths, but for helping herself to her clients' money.

Tried and convicted of fraud in 1973, Matajke was sentenced to five years in prison. She escaped in February 1974 and remained at large until she was recaptured in 1980. She was returned to finish her sentence and despite her escape, won parole in 1983. After her release, Matajke moved to Little Rock, Arkansas, where she again offered her services as a live-in assistant. Her duties in this capacity included cooking for her clients, shopping for them and paying their bills, all of which offered ample opportunity for fraud and murder.

On March 24, 1985, Matajke began caring for Paul Kinsey, 72, and his 71-year-old wife, Opal. She'd barely settled in when Opal died on April 5, her death attributed to cancer. Soon after, Paul Kinsey's health also began to deteriorate. Relatives put it down to grief at the death of his wife.

While Matajke's continued caring for Kinsey, she acquired another elderly client, Marion Doyle. Like Opal Kinsey, Doyle was a cancer sufferer. However, when she died, just nine days after Matajke's arrival, her death was not from that disease but from a drug overdose. This should have aroused suspicion, but the police ruled the death a suicide.

An inventory of Doyle's estate, meanwhile, turned up several suspicious looking checks, totaling $4,000, all made out to Dorothy Matajke. The executor of the estate reported his findings to the police and an exhumation was ordered. As expected, tissue samples showed sufficient drugs to cause death. What was interesting, though, was that some of the drugs in Doyle's system were not medications prescribed to her.

While investigators pondered their next move, Paul Kinsey's health continued to decline. Eventually, he refused to eat meals prepared for him by Matajke. He told relatives that she was poisoning him, but they put it down to the ramblings of an old man. On October 28, he ordered Matajke to leave his house. Three days later he was hospitalized in critical condition.

Dorothy Matajke wasn't about to give up that easily. A couple of days later she showed up at the hospital to visit her ex-employer. It was there that police tracked her down and arrested her on charges of theft and fraud relating to transactions against Marion Doyle's bank account. Subsequent investigation showed that she had also been methodically emptying Paul Kinsey's accounts.

There was more to come. A search of Matajke's home turned up vials of drugs and tranquilizers, along with three jars of arsenic-based ant poison. On November 24, she was arraigned on first-degree murder charges in the death of Marion Doyle and first-degree battery in the poisoning of Paul Kinsey.

An exhumation order was also obtained for Opal Kinsey's body and showed lethal levels of arsenic. When Paul Kinsey died, on February 10, 1987, another charge of first-degree murder was added.

Matajke was eventually sentenced to life plus 60 years for the murders committed in Arkansas. Investigators in Iowa are also looking into the suspicious deaths of five patients who died there while being attended by Dorothy Matajke.

John McRae

On September 9, 1950, Joey Housey failed to return home for supper. The 8-year-old had last been seen playing in a field near his home and an immediate search was launched. It, and the searches carried out over the next few days, turned up no trace of the boy.

Two weeks later, on a Saturday afternoon, volunteers braved the rain to continue searching. As one of them was crossing a field, he sat down for a breather on a concrete block. It was then that he noticed an arm protruding from the mud. It was Joey. He'd been stabbed to death, his throat and genitals slashed with a straight razor.

A few days later, 15-year-old John McRae described to his father a dream in which he'd killed a young boy. The older man immediately saw through his son's ruse and realized that he was confessing to murder. Packed off to relatives in Canada, McRae was soon arrested and brought back to face prosecution. He was tried as an adult, found guilty and sentenced to life in prison.

That should have been the end of the story, but in 1971, McRae's sentence was commuted, making him eligible for parole. That was granted a year later, and on February 2, 1972, the convicted murderer was a free man.

Following his release, McRae remained in Michigan, married and fathered a son. In 1976, with his period of parole completed, he moved to Florida and found work as a prison guard at Brevard Correctional Institute. He was later transferred to a juvenile facility in Brevard County.

In April 1977, Keith Fleming, a 13-year-old surfer, disappeared from Cocoa Beach Pier, in an area where McRae later admitted he liked to "hang out and watch the boys."

In March 1979, 12-year-old Kip Hess was at a church carnival where McRae was moonlighting as a security guard. Kip was a slightly built child and he was being picked on by a group of kids when McRae came to his rescue. McRae had his son, Martin, befriend Kip.

A few days later, Kip left for school and disappeared. A search was launched, with McRae among the concerned volunteers looking for the boy. He was never found.

McRae, meanwhile, had befriended a young man at the correctional facility where he worked. There were rumors of an improper relationship between McRae and 19-year-old Charles Collingwood, but McRae denied this, insisting that Collingwood helped him by informing on other inmates. Then, in December 1979, Collingwood was gone, having apparently escaped from a work detail. Despite an extensive search by law enforcement officers, he was never found.

The police were not convinced that Collingwood had escaped. They believed that McRae had something to do with his disappearance, and as they intensified their focus, McRae suddenly uprooted his family and moved back to Michigan.

He settled in Clare County, where he built a ramshackle compound and began raising angora goats. On September 15, 1987, McRae's 15-year-old neighbor, Randy Laufer, disappeared. Randy's parents reported him missing, but the local police were convinced that he had run away from home and treated the disappearance as a missing person case.

Within months of Randy's disappearance, McRae was on the move again, this time to Arizona, where his mother now lived.

In 1997, the new tenant at the Michigan property that McRae had once occupied was demolishing an old wall constructed during his stay. As the breezeblocks were being removed, the woman noticed a human skull among the rubble. The police were called and an evacuation of the site turned up the skeletal remains of Randy Laufer.

McRae was extradited from Arizona and tried for the Laufer murder in 1998. A guilty verdict saw him sentenced to life in prison. He died there on June 28, 2005, at the age of 70.

The bodies of Keith Fleming, Kip Hess, and Charles Collingwood have never been found, although police in Brevard County insist there is strong evidence linking McRae to their disappearances.

Bruce Mendenhall

Most serial killers show signs of aberrant behavior early in life, whether it be animal cruelty, fire starting, or deviant sexual behavior. Many develop substance abuse problems by their teens and begin racking up a catalog of juvenile arrests. By the time they graduate to murder, most already have a police record.

Bruce Mendenhall was different. The father of two was a regular churchgoer and a caring husband to his diabetic wife. He was in steady employment as a truck driver and had even stood for mayor of his hometown, Albion, Illinois. Sure he could be difficult and argumentative, but no one suspected that there was anything unusual about him. No one, that is, until he was arrested for the murders of six women.

Evidence of Mendenhall's shadowy second life first came to light on July 12, 2007, when a Tennessee police detective went to a truck stop outside of Nashville to question witnesses to a recent homicide. As he parked his car, the detective noticed a truck that matched a vehicle connected to his case. The driver, Bruce Mendenhall, seemed nervous when approached, but gave the officer permission to search his vehicle. He'd barely begun when he found blood spatters in the cab. He then placed Mendenhall under arrest.

A subsequent search of the vehicle turned up a treasure trove of evidence, including a garbage bag containing blood-soaked clothing, a .22 rifle, knives, handcuffs, latex gloves, a nightstick, and a collection of sex toys.

Mendenhall, meanwhile, had been taken in for questioning and although he maintained his innocence his answers were inconsistent. He soon implicated himself in the case the officers were investigating, the murder of prostitute Sara Nicole Hulbert. As the detectives continued probing, he seemed to crumble, confessing to the murders of Hulbert and five other women.

Among the victims were Symantha Winters, a prostitute found shot to death on June 6, 2007, her body dumped in a trash can at a truck stop in Lebanon, Tennessee; Lucille Carter, shot with a .22-caliber weapon and left in a dumpster with a plastic bag taped around her head on July 1; and an unnamed woman killed at the Flying J truck stop in Indianapolis on July 11, 2007.

The police also believe that Mendenhall might be responsible for killing Atlanta prostitute Deborah Ann Glover; Sherry Drinkard, a prostitute from Gary, Indiana, and Carma Purpura, a 31-year old mother of two, who was last seen on July 11, 2007, at an Indianapolis truck stop. Travel logs put Mendenhall at the scenes of each of these crimes and DNA retrieved from items found in his truck provided further corroboration. In addition, Mendenhall was found to be in possession of Pupura's cell phone and ATM card when he was arrested.

Mendenhall would eventually be charged with the Hulbert, Winters, and Purpura murders and sentenced to life in prison. The story does have one more twist, though.

While he was awaiting trial, Mendenhall's wife died, leaving him a substantial life insurance payout. He decided to put this money to good use by attempting to have three of the witnesses against him killed. However, his attempts to enlist two soon-to-be-released inmates resulted in the matter being referred to the authorities. Tried and convicted for conspiracy to commit murder, Mendenhall had an additional 30 years tacked on to his sentence.

Mendenhall remains a murder suspect in Georgia, Illinois, New Mexico, Oklahoma, and Texas.

Roy Mitchell

On May 25, 1922, 21-year-old Harvey Bolton was parked with his girlfriend on a secluded road outside Waco, Texas, when a man emerged from some nearby bushes and walk towards the car. As the man got closer he suddenly raised a pistol and fired three times, hitting Bolton and killing him instantly. He then dragged the woman from the vehicle and raped her, before fleeing the scene.

The rape victim survived and the following day named a local black man, Jesse Thomas, as her assailant. Thomas was then hunted down and shot by the girl's father before his body was carried to a city square and set alight by a chanting mob.

Unfortunately, the young woman had made a grave mistake. Thomas was not the man who had attacked her, a fact made glaringly obvious on November 20.

On that day, 19-year-old Grady Skipworth and his girlfriend, Naomi Boucher, were parked near a local make-out spot called "Lover's Leap," in Cameron Park. As the couple sat in their car, a man emerged from the darkness, and fired at Skipworth with a shotgun, hitting him in the head. He then dragged the body from the car and tossed it over the cliff before returning to attack the terrified woman as she cowered in the vehicle. She too was pushed from the precipice but landed in some trees, which broke her fall and saved her life.

Like the previous victim, Naomi named a black man as her attacker. This time, though, the citizens of Waco let justice take its course. The man was tried and found not guilty by the all-white jury.

On January 10, 1923, a couple was driving through Cameron Park when a man burst from the undergrowth and leapt onto the vehicle's running board. He tried to force the barrel of a shotgun through the passenger window but was shaken off and knocked to the ground before he could fire. By the time the police arrived, the man was long gone. But he'd left something behind, a checkered cap, which was taken into evidence.

Just ten days later, the killer struck again, shooting W.E. Holt in the head, before raping his fiancée Ethel Denecamp and beating her to death. Their car was found abandoned on a Waco street the following morning.

A short while after this latest attack, the police got a break in the case when someone came forward to identify the owner of the cap found at the site of the previous attack. It belonged, he said, to Roy Mitchell, a 30-year-old recently moved to the city from Louisiana.

It was interesting information, but hardly enough to arrest a man for murder. Nonetheless, the police soon had reason to bring Mitchell in, after he was busted for illegal gambling. A search of his home turned up a handgun stolen from another murder victim, plus a fob watch stolen from Grady Skipworth.

Faced with the evidence against him, Mitchell confessed to five murders, including that of William Driskell, a cotton trader and part-time deputy, from whom he'd stolen the pistol.

Mitchell went on trial in March 1923, and despite recanting his earlier confession he was found guilty and sentenced to die. In what was the last public execution in Texas, the hanging took place on July 30, 1923, before a cheering crowd estimated at 8,000.

Henry Lee Moore

Axe murders are all but unheard in the modern era. But in the late 1800's and early 1900's, when most families had an axe lying around to chop firewood, they were all too common. Most often, they resulted from some heated argument, one of the adversaries eventually resorting to making his point with the dull blade of a conveniently located bludgeon.

The murders committed by Henry Lee Moore were different. Moore was a transient, a drifter who wandered the countryside looking for work and was not averse to a bit of petty larceny to supplement his meager earnings. He was also known to have a ferocious temper, and any attempt at resistance was usually met with violence.

On December 17, 1912, police in Columbia, Missouri, were called to the scene of a brutal double murder. Mary Wilson, 82, and her 61-year-old daughter, Georgia Moore, were found hacked and bludgeoned to death in their home. The blows that had killed them were delivered with such force that the victims' brains lay exposed. The murder weapon, a blunt axe with a broken handle, lay close at hand and a suspect was soon in custody. He was Henry Moore, son of one of the victims, grandson of the other.

Moore was tried, found guilty and sentenced to life in prison. That should have been the end of the story. It was barely the beginning.

In March of 1913, the authorities in Villisca, Iowa, requested federal assistance in helping to catch the perpetrator of a massacre carried out in June of 1912. An unidentified assailant had entered the home of J.B. Moore and had axed him to death along with his four children, and two female visitors. The murders had lain unsolved ever since. Villisca lawmen were desperate to solve them.

The federal officer assigned to the case was M.W. McClaughry. He began his investigation by looking for other cases with a similar M.O. and soon found them. Nine months earlier, in September 1911, H.C. Wayne, his wife, and child, along with a Mrs. A.J. Burnham and her children, had been killed in Colorado Springs; in October, three members of the Dewson family had been slain in Monmouth, Illinois; that same month, the Showman family – all five of them – had been hacked to death at their home in Ellsworth, Kansas; on June 5, 1912, just days before the Villisca massacre, Rollin Hudson and his wife were killed in Paola, Kansas. As in the other cases, the police had no leads and no clues as to the identity of the axe man.

McClaughry was convinced that the same man was responsible for all of the murders, but that conclusion brought him no closer to naming a suspect. Then, McClaughry's father, the warden of the federal penitentiary at Leavenworth, passed on some information about a prisoner, Henry Moore, currently serving life in Missouri.

In May, McClaughry traveled to Missouri to interview Moore and as a result of those conversations declared the 23 axe murders solved. Moore would never be tried, though. He remained incarcerated until 1949 when he was released at age 82.

Despite McClaughry's confidence that Henry Moore was responsible for the Villisca murders, the case remains officially unsolved.

Eddie Lee Mosley

Eddie Lee Mosley was born on March 31, 1947, the third of Willie Mae Robinson's 10 children. There were complications with the delivery and from an early age, family members could tell that there was something not right with the boy. That became even more apparent as he aged. In 1960, at age 13, Eddie dropped out of school, after failing again to graduate from the third grade.

By the age of 18, Mosley was a huge, hulking young man who still could not read or write and earned his living as a manual laborer. He had also begun to acquire a lengthy rap sheet, which over the years would grow to include charges ranging from indecent exposure to sexual assault, to murder.

Between November 1971 and July 1973, Fort Lauderdale, Florida, was plagued by a prolific rapist who lured nearly 150 victims to vacant lots, then choked and raped them. Two women had died during the attacks.

Moseley was eventually identified as the attacker after being spotted on the street by one of his victims. He was subsequently picked from a police lineup by over 40 women.

Taken into custody, Moseley admitted to sex with "hundreds" of women but denied that he'd forced any of them. He was eventually tried for only three rapes. Found not guilty by reason of insanity, he was sent to the Florida State Hospital in Chattahoochee, where he would remain for the next five years. With Mosley off the street, the number of rapes in the area dropped immediately.

In June 1979, Mosley was declared cured and released. During the next three months, four young, black women turned up raped and strangled, all within walking distance of Mosley's Fort Lauderdale home.

However, when police eventually announced an arrest, it was not Mosley, but a mentally handicapped man, named Jerry Frank Townsend, who took the rap. Townsend readily confessed to the crimes and was subsequently sentenced to life in prison. Years later, DNA evidence would exonerate Townsend and point the finger at Moseley.

For now, though, Moseley was still at large, and in the next few months (with Townsend safely behind bars) three more bodies were discovered near Moseley's home.

When investigators tried to question Mosley, his family packed him off to live with his grandfather in Lakeland. Within weeks of his arrival there, two young, black women were missing. Their skeletal remains would later be found in open fields, date of death determined to be around the time Moseley lived in the area.

Back in Fort Lauderdale on April 12, 1980, Moseley again fell foul of the law. Convicted on a charge of sexual battery, he was sentenced to 15 years in prison. He served less than three, before being released on November 15, 1983.

A month after Moseley's release, a group of boys found the body of Geraldine Barfield, 35, in a field in northwest Fort Lauderdale. Two weeks later, the corpse of 54-year-old Emma Cook was found in an abandoned house. Cook was found a short time after her death, and a semen sample lifted from the scene would later be matched to Moseley.

In May 1984, and again in October 1985, Mosley found himself in court charged with rape. Each time he walked free. Then, after two more bodies turned up, Fort Lauderdale PD finally turned to the FBI for help. The profile prepared by the Bureau might as well have been an identikit for Eddie Moseley.

Without looking at any suspect information, the VICAP unit described an unmarried, middle-aged black man living in the area of the murders. He would be streetwise, a school dropout with a history of mental illness and below-average intelligence. He would dabble in alcohol and drugs and be a loner who walked the streets at night. He would have been questioned before about the allegations and have denied them.

The Bureau also offered a strategy for questioning the suspect should he be arrested. This would eventually be called into play in 1987, after the raped and strangled body of Santrail Lowe, 24, was found in a junkyard on Northwest Sixth Place.

On the night of May 17, 1987, Moseley was arrested for a break-in at a local nursery. Detectives began interrogating him about the burglary but quickly switched to the murdered women, using the strategy devised by the FBI. Within five hours, they had a confession.

However, rather than bring the case to a close, the confession was only the beginning of a lengthy legal process which eventually saw Moseley declared unfit to stand trial. He is currently incarcerated at the Corrections Mental Health Institution in Chattahoochee, but may one day be released. If he is, homicide detectives are in no doubt that he will kill again.

Francis Nemechek

On the night of December 13, 1974, a man named Francis Nemechek sat atop an overpass on Interstate 70, west of Hays, Kansas. Pressed to his shoulder was a rifle fitted with a sniper scope, now focused on a small car that had just passed in the darkness. Nemechek was an experienced hunter, so when he squeezed the trigger, the bullet found its mark, puncturing one of the vehicle's tires. Nemecheck then got into his truck and drove to the "aid" of the stranded motorists.

Inside the car, he found Cheryl Young, 21, her 19-year-old friend Diane Lovett and Young's son, Guy, 2 years and 10 months old. The three were returning from Colorado, en route to their home in Iowa. Seeing Nemechek approaching, the women got into their car, rolled up the windows and refused his help. Nemechek then went back to his truck, got a shotgun and forced them from their car into his vehicle.

He drove his terrified victims to an abandoned farmhouse on an isolated stretch of road, 15 miles north of I-70. There he raped and shot the two women before leaving, abandoning the toddler to his fate. Guy Lovett's body would be found a month later. An autopsy determined that he'd frozen to death.

Shortly before 1 a.m. on January 1, 1976, a man driving a pickup truck, fired at a family of four traveling eastbound on I-70 near Ogallah. The family managed to escape and reported the incident, leading to Nemechek's arrest. Released on $20,000 bond, he was free until his court appearance, scheduled for September 1976.

On the evening of June 30, 1976, 20-year-old University of Kansas student Carla Baker was riding her bike in Hays, when she encountered Nemechek urinating beside his truck. As she passed, he exposed himself to her and Carla made the fatal mistake of stopping to reprimand him. He overpowered her at knifepoint, drove her to Cedar Bluff Reservoir and tried to rape her. When she resisted, he stabbed her to death. Carla's father found her bicycle beside the road the next morning, but her body would lay undiscovered for months.

The next victim was 16-year-old Paula Fabrizius, a high school senior and cheerleader at Ellis High School. Paula worked part-time as a rangerette at Cedar Bluff Reservoir.

On Saturday, August 21, 1976, Nemechek abducted her from her station and drove her to Castle Rock, a sandstone formation near Quinter, almost 30 miles away. There, he raped and then stabbed the girl to death before throwing her nude body off a 25-foot bluff.

The following day, he participated in a search for Paula's body in the area from which she'd gone missing.

Nemechek must have thought that Paula's body would lay undiscovered indefinitely, but it was found by Rangers the following day. Among the items found near the scene was a warranty card for a citizen's band (CB) radio. When KBI agents processed it, they discovered that it carried a distinct thumbprint.

That print turned out to belong to Francis Nemechek. The case against Nemechek was strengthened further when several eyewitnesses reported seeing his truck at the reservoir on the day of the murder.

On August 24, 1976, KBI agents charged Nemechek with the murder of Paula Fabrizius. A month later Carla Baker's remains were found in a canyon near Cedar Bluff Reservoir and Nemechek's jailhouse boasts about the murders of Fabrizius, Baker, Lovett and Young saw him charged with those crimes, as well as the murder of Guy Young.

Nemechek was found guilty on all five counts and sentenced to five life terms. He is currently an inmate at Lansing Correctional Facility in Kansas.

Alfredo R. Prieto

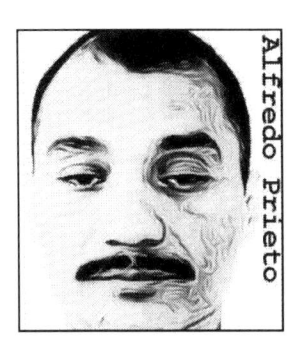

'Dead man walking' is a term popularly applied to death row inmates. Yet in the state of California, it might as well be, 'dead man waiting,' such are the long delays between the passing of a death penalty and its eventual execution. The reason for these delays lies in California's notoriously complex statutes, which allow inmates to lodge appeal after appeal, thus postponing their date with the executioner. Postponements often run to decades, and unless California legislators have an unlikely change of heart and embark on an execution jamboree, many death sentences will eventually be commuted to life in prison.

In 2008, one of those awaiting execution at San Quentin was Alfredo R. Prieto, condemned to die for the rape and murder of 15-year-old Yvette Woodruff. The murder occurred on September 2, 1990. On that day, Prieto and two other men broke into a house in

Ontario, California, intent on burglary. Finding three women inside, the men decided instead to rape them.

Prieto focused his attentions on Yvette, sexually assaulting her before shooting her in the head. His accomplices raped and then stabbed the other two women. The men then departed, leaving their victims for dead. Fortunately, the two stab victims survived and were eventually able to point the finger at their assailants. Yvette, though, was dead at the scene and her murder would lead to Prieto's conviction and death sentence.

Prieto was surly and uncooperative at his trial, barely responding when the death sentence was read out. No doubt he was aware that "death" in California means "life with death row benefits," and he settled into San Quentin while his lawyers began working on the laborious appeals process.

This was still ongoing five years later when cold case investigators on the other side of the country began looking into a brutal rape and double homicide. On December 3, 1988, Rachael Raver and Warren Fulton III, both 22, had had dinner with Fulton's parents, before going to a bar in Fairfax, Virginia. They left shortly after midnight and weren't seen until their bodies were found in an empty lot two days later.

Fulton had been shot in the back and Raver, whose nude body was found nearby, had died of a similar wound. Investigators theorized that the couple had been taken to the lot at gunpoint and that Raver had been forced to disrobe. The assailant had then turned the gun on Fulton and Raver had made a run for it. Running terrified through the dark, she'd covered only a short distance when the attacker caught up with her, shot her in the back and then raped her as she lay dying.

The case had lain unsolved for seven years, but in 2005, cold case investigators submitted evidence from the crime scene for DNA analysis and got a match. It led them to death row inmate Alfredo R. Prieto.

Prieto was duly charged and extradited to Virginia to face trial. Despite his California conviction, the Commonwealth was determined to try him for the Fulton / Raver murders. As Commonwealth's Attorney Raymond F. Morrogh explained. "He'll never get the death penalty in California. He effectively has a life sentence. I think it's time to bring him to justice for his horrible crimes."

On November 5, 2010, a Fairfax County judge sentenced Prieto to death for the murders of Rachael Raver and Warren Fulton. Prieto has since been linked by DNA and ballistic evidence to six other murders in Virginia and California: Veronica Jefferson in 1988; Manuel Sermeno in 1989; plus two double homicides in 1990, Stacey Siegrist and Tony Gianuzzi, and Lula and Herbert Farley.

Prieto currently resides on death row at Sussex State Prison in Waverly, Virginia. Unlike California, Virginia typically executes condemned murderers within five to seven years.

Larry Ralston

On September 24, 1977, three 15-year-old girls from Price Hill, Ohio, were hitchhiking to a movie when a man stopped to give them a lift. The man promised to drop them off at the movie theater but instead drove them to an isolated road in Clermont County. There, he stopped the car, with the passenger side up against an embankment, preventing the girls' escape. Over the next two hours, he repeatedly raped them. They escaped only when their assailant was distracted by an approaching car.

On November 10, 1977, a man named Larry Ralston was arrested and charged with the rapes. As Investigator Bob Stout was transporting Ralston to the Clermont County Jail in Batavia, the captive suddenly started crying. "I didn't mean to kill any of them," he blubbered, which left Stout both perplexed and terrified. Ralston hadn't been charged with killing anyone.

Over the next two weeks, a series of grueling interrogations finally provided investigators with a confession to a series of brutal serial killings that had left them baffled for over two years.

The first murder had been committed on September 3, 1975. Linda Kay Harmon, 17, recently arrived in town, left home to attend her first day of school at Withrow High. She was last seen waiting for a bus at Wolfangle Road and Beechmont Avenue, some three blocks from her home. Then she seemed to have disappeared into thin air.

Just over a month later, a resident of nearby Felicity Ohio, was horrified when his dogs brought home a decomposed human arm. The police were called and a search of the nearby woods yielded the rest of Linda Kay Harmon's remains.

Almost a year later, on November 15, 1976, hunters in Clermont County discovered the nude remains of a young woman. The victim was identified as 23-year-old Nancy Grigsby of Withamsville. Nancy had gone missing on May 4, 1976, after leaving a bar in Mount Lookout, to meet her boyfriend in Fairfax.

And the corpses kept showing up over the months that followed. Fifteen-year-old Elaina Marie Bear of Northside was found on February 28, 1977, her body discarded in a creek bed off Katy's Lane near Wilmington in Clinton County. Diana Sue McCrobie, 16, of Springfield Township, was found October 22, 1977. Her body had been covered with brush at East Fork Lake State Park in Clermont County. She had once dated Larry Ralston.

So far the police had Ralston on four homicides and a further indictment would later be added with the discovery of Mary Ruth Hopkins' body on June 30, 1976. The 21-year-old was naked, except for a T-shirt knotted around her neck when she was found, just off Five Mile Road in Anderson Township.

In a chilling taped confession, Ralston recalled how he picked up his hitchhiking victims, then drove them around, drinking wine and smoking marijuana. Eventually, he'd stop in an isolated spot and demand sex. If the woman refused, he'd strangle her, then drive home to listen to his favorite song, "Fly Like An Eagle." The music put him into a sort of trance, he said.

Ralston faced several trials related to his murder spree, eventually earning three life terms and one death sentence (for the murder of Elaina Marie Bear). The sentence was eventually commuted to life in 1978, after the U.S. Supreme Court declared the death penalty unconstitutional.

Ralston's conviction in the Nancy Grigsby murder was subsequently overturned. He is currently incarcerated at Chillicothe Correctional Institution in Ohio.

Robert Reldan

On the afternoon of August 9, 1974, Mary Pryor, 17, and Lorraine Kelly, 16, left Pryor's home in North Bergen, New Jersey, on their way to do some shopping. On August 10, they were officially reported missing and four days later, their bodies were found in a wooded area near Montvale. They'd been raped and strangled.

Police believed that the girls had been hitchhiking and had been picked up by their killer. However, following that line of inquiry got investigators no closer to solving the murders.

On December 13, 1974, two more teenagers disappeared. Doreen Carlucci, age 14, and 15-year-old Joanne Delardo were last seen at a church youth center in Woodbridge. Their bodies were found in Manalapan Township two weeks later. The girls had both been raped and beaten, with death attributed to ligature strangulation.

The next victim was 26-year-old Susan Reynes, abducted from her Haworth, New Jersey, home on October 6, 1975. Eight days later, 22-year-old Susan Reeve vanished while walking from a bus stop to her home in Demarest. Both were still missing when Denise Evans and Carolyn Hedgepeth, both 15, disappeared in Wilmington, Delaware, on October 24. Their bodies were found the following day in Salem County, New Jersey. Both had died from bullet wounds to the back of the head.

On October 27, a patrolman driving along a stretch of highway in Rockland County, New York, spotted an arrow etched into an embankment alongside the word "Reeve." Aware that Susan Reeve had been reported missing, he called it in. A search of the area yielded Susan's strangled corpse. The following day, Susan Reynes, missing since October 6, was found some seven miles away. She, too, had been strangled.

Despite the varying methods employed in the murders, police were now of the opinion that they were hunting a serial killer, although they had no idea who he might be. Then, on October 31, 1975, a suspect fell into their laps.

Robert Reldan, an ex-con from Tenafly, New Jersey, had been arrested on a charge of burglary in Closter. Reldan had a long rap sheet, including rape and assault with a deadly weapon. He'd served various prison terms before being declared "rehabilitated," and released from Rahway prison in May 1975. So impressed were the prison authorities with Reldan's progress that they chose him to be interviewed on television by David Frost, as a testament to the success of their program.

Aware of Reldan's record as a sex offender, detectives questioned him about the Reeve and Reynes murders. On November 2, they confidently declared that he was "not the man." Further evidence led them to change their minds. In January 1977, Reldan was indicted on two counts of murder.

More trouble followed for Reldan. In April 1977, he was charged with conspiracy, for trying to arrange a hit on a wealthy aunt from inside prison. Unfortunately for Reldan, the "hitman" he tried to hire was an undercover cop. Convicted of conspiracy in June 1978, Reldan was sentenced to a term of 20 to 50 years in prison.

Reldan's murder trial eventually came to court in October 1978. However, the multiple murderer had no intention of going through with it. On October 15, he used a concealed key to unlock his handcuffs. He then sprayed Mace into a guard's face and made a dash for freedom. He was at large for mere hours, during which he crashed a stolen car into a ditch and ended up in hospital.

The trial resumed the following day and concluded with guilty verdicts in the murders of Susan Reynes and Susan Reeve. Reldan was sentenced to life in prison. He has never been charged with the other six murders, although he remains the only suspect.

Marc Sappington

To the officers who interrogated him, Marc Sappington was an enigma, an intelligent, articulate, even cheerful, young man, who was somehow possessed of a compulsion to consume human flesh and drink human blood. This obsession, fueled by Sappington's PCP addiction, would eventually lead to the grisly deaths of four people, three of them close friends of the "Kansas City Vampire."

Sappington grew up on the north side of Kansas City. His father deserted the family before his birth and his mother worked hard to raise her son in the best possible way. Dirt poor, they found solace in their local church, where Sappington sang in the choir.

At school, he was an average student who was admired by teachers and classmates nonetheless for his engaging personality. Dig below the surface, however, and a different Marc Sappington emerged. He was a habitual PCP user, a habit that had already led him down the path of petty larceny.

Still, none of his crimes were directed against people. Not at least, until March 16, 2001.

On that day, Sappington and a local street thug named Armando Gaitan, held up a man named David Marshak at gunpoint. They demanded cash and Marshak immediately complied, handing over his wallet. However, his co-operation did not save him. For some inexplicable reason, Sappington opened fire, killing Marshak instantly.

After the murder, Gaitan fled to Texas, while Sappington stayed in Kansas City and used the money he'd stolen to go on a PCP binge. Perhaps it was the drugs or perhaps the schizophrenia with which he was later diagnosed, but he began to become obsessed with the idea of eating flesh and drinking blood. He'd later tell investigators that the voices in his head told him to do so, and promised severe punishments if he did not comply.

On April 7, 2001, Sappington showed up at the home of lifelong friend, Terry Green, 25. Talking Green down to the basement, Sappington picked up a hunting knife and attacked, the assault launched with such ferocity, that the blade entered Green's back and exited his chest.

With his friend lying crumpled on the floor, Sappington knelt down and lapped at the blood flowing from multiple wounds. He then loaded the body into Green's mother's car and drove to a nightclub that he and Green had often frequented. There, he dumped the corpse in the parking lot.

Three days later, according to Sappington, the voices instructed him to kill again. The victim he chose was another friend, 22-year-old Michael Weaver.

Walking past Weaver's house, Sappington saw his friend sitting on the porch and persuaded him to go for a ride. He then told Weaver to stop in an alley so that they could do some drugs. Weaver had barely brought the car to a halt when Sappington turned on him and stabbed him to death.

Leaving Weaver's body in the car, Sappington walked towards his home, just a few blocks away. On the way there, he encountered Alton Brown, a teenager who looked up to him as an older brother. Luring Brown into his house, he killed him with a blast from a shotgun, then drank some of his blood. He went even further this time, slicing some flesh from Brown's leg, frying and eating it.

Without even bothering to conceal the corpse, Sappington left the house. Brown's body was discovered by Sappington's mother hours later. She immediately called the police.

It didn't take long for the cops to find Sappington. After a brief chase during which he kidnapped a female driver and commandeered her vehicle, he was arrested.

Brought to trial in July 2004, his insanity defense was rejected by the jury. He was sentenced to four terms of life imprisonment.

Jason Scott

At around 2 a.m. on Monday, January 26, 2009, the 911 dispatcher in Largo, Maryland, received a desperate phone call. In whispered tones, the female caller said that she and her mother had been shot by an intruder to their home. Obtaining the address, the dispatcher immediately sent a unit to the 10800 block of Southall Drive, where they found Karen Lofton, 45, and her 16-year-old daughter, Karissa, shot to death. Karissa had been the one who placed the call.

There appeared to be no forced entry to the house and nothing appeared to have been stolen, leaving police baffled as to the motive for the killings. Largo is a quiet town where violent crime is rare. Yet, just 12 days earlier another homicide had occurred in nearby Upper Marlboro and the police chief found himself fielding questions about a serial killer on the loose. He categorically discounted that possibility.

Less than two months later, at approximately 4 a.m. on Monday, March 16, 2009, firefighters were called to the scene of a car fire. A vehicle was ablaze in the driveway of a vacant house, the fire so intense that it melted the tar beneath it.

It looked like a case of arson and once the flames had been doused and the charred metal had cooled, fire department investigators began scouring the vehicle for clues. They were shocked to find two bodies in the destroyed Nissan Maxima, one lying on the back seat, the other stuffed into the trunk. Although burned beyond recognition, the victims would be identified as Delores Dewitt, 42, and her daughter, Ebony, 20.

With this latest double homicide, the quiet community of Largo was thrown into panic. Four people had been killed in the space of just two months. In addition, the community had recently been plagued by a rash of break-ins and home invasions. Action was demanded and the beleaguered police chief was forced to re-evaluate his earlier assessment. This latest outrage bore startling similarities to the Lofton murders. Perhaps there was a serial killer loose on the streets of Largo after all.

A few months later, ATF agents were in Largo investigating a seemingly unrelated crime, the theft of 26 firearms from a federally licensed gun store on May 26, 2009. Acting on a tip-off, the agents set up a sting and arrested a man named Jason Thomas Scott, who was selling guns from the parking lot of the local UPS depot.

With Scott in custody, the agents obtained a warrant to search his home. They got more than they bargained for. Aside from the stolen firearms, there was evidence of an extensive and meticulously planned crime spree. The police found burglary tools, a rape kit, restraints, a police scanner, and numerous items stolen from homes in the area. They also found a pornographic videotape of a local teenager. The girl had been forced to strip and pose for a man who had broken into her home a few months earlier. Now the police knew who that man was.

Scott, it turned out, was a part-time employee of UPS, and had been using their computer system to identify potential targets. Evidence was soon obtained that linked him to the two double homicides as well as at least 25 burglaries and nine home invasions. He was also linked to another murder, that of 46-year-old Vilma Butler, shot to death in her home in June 2008.

The evidence was overwhelming and Scott faced the very real possibility of the death penalty. In an effort to avoid this, he lodged an Alford plea. This unusual legal maneuver means that the defendant acknowledges that the state has sufficient evidence to convict, but stops short of admitting to the crimes.

On January 11, 2012, Jason Scott was sentenced to 100 years in prison for the Largo murders. A further 85 years was added in 2013 for the murder of Vilma Butler.

William Smith

On February 19, 1984, 21-year-old Rebecca Darling was working the graveyard shift at an all-night convenience store in Salem, Oregon, when she disappeared. She was there at 3:20 a.m. when a customer came in to make a purchase, but when another customer arrived about 30 minutes later, he found the store standing empty and unattended. The man called the police, who launched an immediate search of the area.

Neither that search, nor the larger effort conducted over the following days, was able to find the missing woman. Her decomposed remains eventually showed up over a month later, on March 25. She'd been concealed in bushes along the Little Pudding River, six miles northeast of town. Nude from the waist up, and with her hands tied behind her back, it was obvious that she'd been the victim of a sexual assault. Cause of death also appeared obvious, a length of rope was still knotted around her neck.

A couple of weeks after the discovery of the body, police responded to reports of an abandoned car. The vehicle was traced to a University of Oregon student who said that she'd lent it to a friend, 18-year-old co-ed Katherine Redmond. Redmond had last been seen at 2:15 a.m. when she'd driven away from a frat party. Her nude body was found on April 11, just four miles from where Rebecca Darling had been discovered. She'd been strangled and her vagina had been lacerated by some unknown foreign object. Witnesses reported a late-1960s Pontiac station wagon parked in the area where Redmond may have encountered her killer.

As police continued their inquiries, another young woman reported having been bumped by a similar car. The driver had then offered her a ride but had quickly driven off when she said her car was okay and suggested they both drive to a nearby gas station to exchange insurance details.

Based on the woman's descriptions of the driver and vehicle, the police soon focused their attention on William Smith, a high school dropout and unemployed short order cook. Smith had a lengthy rap sheet that included arrests for burglary, sexual assault, and "menacing." He'd also been questioned about the murder of a 14-year-old girl in Boise, Idaho. He had returned to his hometown of Salem shortly before Rebecca Darling's murder.

Arrested on April 26, 1984, Smith was arraigned on two counts of first-degree murder, his trial set for July. He was released on bail until then.

On July 4, 1982, Sherry Eyerly, a delivery woman for Domino's Pizza, disappeared. The 18-year-old's car was found with the engine still running, the three pizzas she'd been delivering placed on the ground near her vehicle. Sherry, though, was nowhere to be seen. A massive search over the days and weeks that followed failed to find her.

While that search was ongoing, Smith went on trial for the Darling and Redmond murders and was found guilty on both counts, drawing two consecutive terms of life imprisonment.

Twenty-five years passed with William Smith securely behind bars. In 2007, cold case investigators began looking again at the Eyerly murder. Most often, these cases are solved by DNA or other forensic evidence, but because Eyerly was never found, such evidence did not exist. Investigators were, however, interested in the similarities between Eyerly's disappearance and two similar cases that had occurred at the time. The more they looked at it, the more they became convinced that Smith was their man.

Eventually, detectives confronted Smith about the murder and he confessed. The mystery of the missing body was also resolved. Smith said that he had dumped the body in the same area as the other victims. However, heavy rains at that time had caused flooding and the corpse had likely been washed away.

In terms of a plea agreement, an additional life term was added to the two William Smith was already serving.

Gary Taylor

Seldom can there have been a man more intent on wreaking violence against women that Gary Taylor. The Michigan native, born in 1936, spent most of his early life in St. Petersburg, Florida, and it was there that he carried out his first attacks. His M.O. was to loiter around bus stops after dark, waiting for a lone woman to attack with a hammer or wrench. One such attack, when Taylor was 18, saw him savagely beat a woman after she disembarked from a bus. Arrested for the crime, he was inexplicably acquitted.

In 1957, Taylor moved back to Detroit. Now 21, he had refined his method and took to driving the streets of the Detroit suburb of Royal Oak, taking pot shots at random women. Four women were wounded, although fortunately none of them died.

Billed the "Royal Oak Sniper" by the media, Taylor was eventually captured and confined to Michigan's Ionia State Hospital. Three years later, he was transferred to the Lafayette Clinic in Detroit. He'd spend the next 11 years shuttling back and forth between several such facilities.

Despite a psychiatrist testifying that Taylor was "unreasonably hostile toward women," he continued to receive passes from the facility. On one such furlong, he forced his way into a woman's home and raped her. On another, he threatened a woman and her daughter with an 18-inch butcher knife. He was not tried for either incident. Instead, he was turned loose as an outpatient, his psychiatrist declaring that he wasn't dangerous as long as he stayed off the booze and called in regularly at the hospital for medication and check-ups.

Soon after his release in 1972, Taylor married and moved with his new wife to Onsted, Michigan. The marriage would be short-lived. By 1973, Taylor had hit the road to Washington. By the time he was reported as a fugitive, 14 months later, he had murdered at least four women in three different states.

Two of the victims, 25-year-old Lee Fletcher and 23-year-old Deborah Heneman, had been killed before Taylor left Michigan. Their bodies would later be found, wrapped in plastic and buried in the backyard of his former residence in Onsted.

Taylor claimed his next known victim in Seattle, Washington, on November 27, 1973. Young housewife, Vonnie Stuth, was abducted from her home and killed.

Investigators eventually tracked Taylor to Enumclaw, Washington, where he answered questions about the Stuth disappearance but refused to sit a polygraph. Unfortunately, Taylor had still not been listed as a fugitive on the NCIC computer and the officers had no reason to hold him. By the time they realized he was wanted in Michigan, Taylor had slipped the net.

He showed up next in Houston, Texas, managing to stay out of the clutches of the law until May 1975, when he was picked up on three charges of sexual assault. These included the rape of a pregnant 16-year-old girl. While being questioned about the rapes, Taylor surprised investigators by confessing to four murders, including Lee Fletcher, Deborah Heneman and Vonnie Stuth. The fourth victim was 21-year-old Susan Houston, an exotic dancer who had gone missing months before.

Following up on the information in Taylor's confession, officers in Michigan unearthed the bodies of Fletcher and Heneman from the grounds of Taylor's former home. Vonnie Stuth was found buried behind the house he'd rented in Enumclaw.

Convicted on the four counts to which he confessed, Taylor was sentenced to life without parole. He remains a suspect in at least 20 unsolved homicides in Michigan, Texas, and California.

Michael Terry

On a chilly evening in December 1985, an unidentified corpse was discovered in Dean Rusk Park, in Atlanta, Georgia. The young, black man had his pants pulled down around his ankles and had been shot several times in the head, death having occurred within the previous 6 hours. With no identification on the corpse, the victim was checked into the morgue as a John Doe and remained that way for four days, until his girlfriend reported him missing and identified the body.

Positive identification now confirmed, detectives began tracing Brown's last movements. They eventually tracked him to a local tavern where he was reported to have left in the company of another black customer, a 300-pound giant of a man known as "Big Mike." However, detectives could find no trace of Mike and the trail soon went cold.

Ten months passed without progress in the case. Then, in mid-October 1986, the body of another young black man was discovered. This time, the corpse had been hidden in an abandoned house and was severely decomposed when found.

Something about the crime scene struck a chord with investigators. The victim had been left with his pants around his ankles and had been shot in the head. An identification soon followed. He was Daryl Williams, a 21-year-old drifter from Ohio. He'd last been seen alive at a bar, on October 5. Then came the news the investigative team was afraid of. The gun that had killed Williams was the same one that had killed Curtis Brown. There was a serial killer loose on the streets of Atlanta.

Within days, another victim was added to the list. George Willingham had left his home on October 5, to run an errand. He was found the next day shot in the back of the head with a .38, the same weapon that had been used on Brown and Williams.

Hunting for clues in the case, detectives began looking at other unsolved homicides that might fit the profile. They turned up two, Alvin George, 31, from Columbus, Ohio; and Jason McColley, 18, an Atlanta native. Both were known street hustlers, who'd been stabbed to death earlier that year. This was of course, different to the M.O. of the other murders, although detectives noted that the shooting victims had also been cut, albeit post-mortem.

As the investigation progressed, the police learned of another link between the killings. Jason McColley had been seen in the company of "Big Mike" on the night of his death. It was too much of a coincidence to ignore. "Big Mike" (real name, Michael Terry) was eventually tracked to the tire-capping shop where he worked and taken into custody. In his possession, police found an unlicensed .357 magnum.

Terry had no problem confessing to the killings, but he claimed that they'd been committed in self-defense. According to him, he'd met the victims in various bars and had left with them to engage in homosexual sex. Afterwards, the men had all threatened violence or robbery. He'd then killed them to protect himself.

Given that Terry towered over all of his victims and considerably outweighed them, it was an unlikely story.

The jury certainly wasn't buying it. Tried for the murders of Curtis Brown and Richard Williams, Terry was found guilty and sentenced to life in prison.

Louise Vermilyea

In October 1911, Chicago police officer, Arthur Bisonette, died suddenly. His death came as a shock to his family and to colleagues at the police department. The 26-year-old had until recently seemed in perfect health.

In fact, it was only after he'd moved into a boarding house run by a woman named Louise Vermilyea that Arthur had fallen ill, complaining of stomach cramps and numbness in the extremities. Bisonette's father recalled that he too, had developed a stomach ailment after dining with his son at the boarding house. His host, Louise Vermilyea, had sprinkled something on his food. When Bisonette asked what it was, Vermilyea replied, "White pepper."

Bisonette Sr. passed this information on to Chicago detectives who requested an autopsy on Arthur Bisonette. It revealed copious amounts of arsenic and in short order, Mrs. Vermilyea found herself in police custody on suspicion of murder. Meanwhile, investigators began looking into the woman's background and found an alarming number of unexplained deaths.

The first occurred in 1893, when Fred Brinkamp, Louise Vermilyea's first husband, died at the family farm near Barrington, Illinois. He was sixty years old at the time, so his death was not considered unusual. His passing left his widow wealthier by $5,000. Louise was to receive two additional insurance payouts soon after, when her two young daughters Cora, 8, and Florence, 5, died of mystery ailments.

In January 1906, another member of the Brinkamp clan, Fred's 26-year-old granddaughter Lillian, died in Chicago, her death attributed to "acute nephritis."

Louise, meanwhile, had remarried. Her new spouse, Charles Vermilyea, lasted just three years before he fell victim to a sudden illness in 1909, leaving Louise

$1,000 better off. Louise was probably disappointed by this windfall, because she soon announced that she planned to sell a house that her husband had owned at Crystal Lake. Harry Vermilyea, Charles's son by a previous marriage, opposed the sale but wasn't around long enough to prevent it. He died shortly after being involved in a blazing row with Louise.

In 1910, Louise was once more in the money after she inherited $1,200 on the death of her 23-year-old son Frank Brinkamp. On his deathbed, Frank confided in his fiancé, Elizabeth Nolan, that he believed his mother had poisoned him, as well as other members of the Brinkamp family. After the young woman repeated these accusations, Louise diverted her murderous attentions from her family, to her acquaintances.

On January 15, 1910, Jason Ruppert, a railroad fireman, became ill after dining with Louise. He died two days later and was followed to the grave soon after by Richard Smith, a train conductor who rented rooms in the Vermilyea household. Smith's room in the boarding house was taken over by Arthur Bisonette, whose death would bring about Vermilyea's downfall.

The motive for these later homicides is unclear, as Louise did not benefit financially by them. However, local mortician E.N. Blocks provided one possible explanation. He said that Louise was obsessed with death and would often show up at his business and offer to help with preparing bodies for burial. She also appeared to have the inside track on deaths in the community and would sometimes be waiting at the deceased's house by the time the undertaker arrived.

Louise Vermilyea, meanwhile, was under house arrest while the bodies of her victims were exhumed for autopsy. She continued to deny involvement in their deaths, claiming, "I simply have been unfortunate in having people dying around me."

On November 4, she collapsed and was rushed to hospital where it was discovered that she had ingested arsenic. She remained bedridden until December 9, when she eventually died, the final victim of her deadly poisoning campaign.

Alexander Watson Jr.

On October 8, 1986, Anne Arundel detectives were called to the home of 34-year-old Boontem Anderson in the Four Seasons neighborhood of Gambrills, Maryland. Boontem had been ill that day and had stayed home from her job at Fort Meade. Later that afternoon, her fiancé's 11-year-old son had returned from school to find her nude body in the bathtub. She'd been stabbed and strangled and (as a later examination would prove) sexually assaulted. Swabs were taken from the body and stored as evidence, but the investigation went nowhere. Soon, it was considered a cold case.

Eighteen months later, on May 23, 1988, Elaine Shereika, 37, went out for a jog before work and never returned. Later that day, a farmer found her blood-soaked body sprawled in his rye field. She'd been raped, beaten, and stabbed before her killer strangled her to death. Once more swabs were taken. Once again they got investigators no closer to catching the killer.

Despite the murders occurring in the same area, there was nothing to connect them. Neither did the murder of 14-year-old Lisa Haenel, occurring as it did over four years later, appear to be part of a series. Lisa, a ninth-grader at Old Mill High School, left her Glen Burnie home on January 15, 1993. When she didn't return her mother's boyfriend went looking for her and found her body the next morning, near a path she used to take to school.

Lisa had not been sexually assaulted, so no swabs were taken from her body. However, detectives did find evidence at the scene – an unsmoked cigarette that turned out to have Lisa's blood on it, as well as her killer's saliva.

The case remained unsolved until 1998, when it landed on the desk of Sgt. David Waltemeyer, the country's first cold case investigator. Waltermeyer submitted the physical evidence for DNA analysis. Year after year, as DNA technology improved, the cases were resubmitted until finally in October 2004, a full profile was extracted and a hit was obtained from the CODIS system. The DNA was from Alexander Watson Jr. and he wasn't difficult to find – he was currently serving life without parole for another murder.

Debra Cobb, a 37-year-old mother of two had been stabbed to death at an office in Forestville. Watson had worked in the same building and he was soon arrested. Copping a plea to avoid the death penalty, he'd been sentenced to life without parole in

December 1994. He was currently behind bars at the Maryland House of Correction in Jessup.

The temptation to approach Watson immediately was strong but cold case investigators held back until they were able to put him in the frame for the three unsolved murders.

Looking into his history they learned that Watson's family had moved to the Four Seasons area in 1985 and that he had lived just doors away from two of the victims, Anderson and Shereika. He also knew the family of Boontem Anderson's fiancée and had worked at a fast food restaurant with her son. Watson would have been just 16 years old at the time of the Anderson murder.

Watson was charged with three counts of first-degree murder in 2004. Having obtained the approval of the victims' families, prosecutors offered a deal, life in prison in exchange for a guilty plea to each murder. Already serving life without parole, Watson had little to lose by accepting. He was sentenced to three consecutive life terms on August 16, 2007.

Dennis Duane Webb

A brutish biker from northeast Texas, Webb committed his first murder at 21, killing the victim simply because he believed the man to be gay. That same year he killed another man as part of his initiation to a biker gang, and later became the gang's chief gunman, responsible for carrying out contract killings. In the years that followed, he killed a number of people during home invasion robberies. He also once gunned down a black man simply because of his race.

The law eventually caught up with Webb in Utah in 1981, when he was convicted of robbery and aggravated kidnapping. However, a plea bargain saw him serve just five and a half years before he was paroled in December 1986. Within two months of his release, the leniency of the Utah parole board would result in the destruction of a young family.

On the night of February 4, 1987, Webb broke into a home in Atascadero, California. His intention was robbery, but after finding John Rainwater, 25, and his 22-year-old wife Lori at home, he struck on a new plan. He decided to spend the night raping and torturing the young couple instead.

After pistol-whipping the Rainwaters into submission, Webb bound and gagged the couple, using nylon stockings, duct tape, and belts. The bonds were so tight that they drew blood, but that was the least of John and Lori's torments. Over the next seven hours, they were repeatedly raped, sodomized, and beaten so savagely that blood would later be found spattered on walls, drapes, and furnishings.

At around six in the morning, the couple somehow managed to work themselves loose and tried to escape. Unfortunately, they never made it. Webb caught them at the front door, shooting John Rainwater in the head and chest at close range, firing a single bullet into the back of Lori's head. He then dragged the bodies back into the bedroom before leaving.

Investigators who arrived on the scene later in the day found a scene of unprecedented carnage. There was blood everywhere, drag marks on the floor, spatters on the walls and drapes. Furnishings and glassware had been deliberately smashed and lay scattered around. In the midst of the chaos, the Rainwater's 15-month-old daughter clung to her mother's naked, lifeless body. Her 7-day-old baby brother lay beside her. Although filthy, bloodied and covered in broken glass, the children were unharmed.

The police were quite obviously desperate to solve the brutal double homicide, but despite the chaos of the crime scene they found few concrete leads. Two months went by without any progress in the case. Then, in April 1987, Dennis Webb's former girlfriend came forward to point the finger at him.

Webb was taken into custody and readily admitted to the killings. However, when investigators pressed him on whether he'd acted alone, he clammed up.

Detectives were, in fact, certain that Webb had had an accomplice and they also believed they knew who he was, even though they lacked the evidence to charge him. (The point was rendered mute soon after when the suspect died while a patient at Patton State Hospital.)

Webb, meanwhile, went on trial for burglary, robbery, and two counts of first-degree murder, the prosecution deciding not to pursue sexual assault charges.

During the sentencing phase, Webb was given a chance to speak and shocked the court by whipping off his shirt and pointing to various tattoos that commemorated the many murders he'd committed. He begged the jury for the death penalty and they were happy to oblige, deliberating for just ninety minutes before granting his wish.

Webb laughed as his sentence was read in August 1988. He currently resides on death row at San Quentin.

Robert Wirth

During late 1987 and early 1988, a particularly vicious serial killer was preying on the elderly women of Milwaukee, Wisconsin. The home-invading fiend broke into his victim's houses and attacked them while they slept, beating and stabbing them into submission. Cause of death in most cases, though, was asphyxiation.

The killer delivered his death sentence in brutal fashion. His M.O. was to force his boot down on his frail victim's throats, crushing their windpipes under his weight. There were other clues too, that pointed to the same perpetrator. The method of entry was consistent and the homes were all ransacked and left in a state of disarray.

The police had a pattern, but what they didn't have was a suspect. And with the rate at which the murderer was committing his killings, the case became the number one priority for Wisconsin homicide investigators. It seemed that barely a week passed without a new victim turning up. Already, the homicidal burglar had killed seven. A break in the case was desperately needed.

When the breakthrough eventually did come, it was from a most unusual source, a toy donkey at the home of the killer's latest victim, a Mrs. Breshnahan. As crime scene investigators were processing the scene, detectives brought in a relative of the victim and asked her to walk through the house and report on anything that seemed out of place. The relative remarked immediately that the toy donkey had been moved. Usually, it was placed on a chair. Now it was on the couch.

The detective picked up the toy and noticed a smear of blood on the fabric. He assumed that the blood was from the victim. Nonetheless, he bagged the toy into evidence and sent it to the Wisconsin State Crime Laboratory for processing.

When the results were returned, the investigating officers could barely contain their excitement. The blood was not from the victim, which meant that it was more than likely from the killer. Moreover, the lab was able to extract a full DNA profile.

Now began the laborious task of finding a match and as the investigative team began submitting the profile to various databases, they prepared themselves for a long wait. Matches back then were not as easily obtained as today. Chances were, their suspect was not even in the database.

A couple of months after the Breshnahan homicide, a man tried to rob a cab driver at gunpoint. Unfortunately for him, the cabbie fought back, overpowered him, and took the gun away. He then called the police. The would-be assailant's name was Robert Wirth, and the gun that he'd used in the attempted robbery had been reported stolen by its owner. It had been taken from a residence next door to one of the murder victims.

Wirth initially refused to submit a blood sample for DNA analysis, doing so only after a warrant was issued. His sample was then compared to the blood lifted from the toy donkey. It was a match.

Robert Wirth went on trial for multiple counts of murder in 1991 and was found guilty, largely on the basis of the DNA evidence against him. Wisconsin does not have the death penalty so he pulled the next best thing, four consecutive life terms plus 20 years.

Martha Wise

Martha Wise was born in 1884 in Hardscrabble, Ohio, one of four children of Fred and Sophie Hasel. She was a big-boned and somewhat slow-witted child, who matured into a dull and unattractive woman. It was fully expected that she'd end up a spinster, but in 1906, she met Albert Wise at a box social. Albert, twenty years Martha's senior, was impressed enough to propose. The two were married soon after.

However, if Martha had any romantic notions about marriage, they were soon dispelled. Her husband was a cruel man who treated her like a farmhand. She was expected to plow the fields and tend the hogs, risking a beating if she complained. Albert did, however, find the time to impregnate his wife five times. The first baby, Albert Jr., died in childhood, the next four - Lester, Everett, Gertrude, and Kenneth – all survived. Not that they were any comfort to their mother. They merely added to her workload.

With such a hard and joyless life to endure, it is unsurprising that Martha sought diversions. The pastime she chose, though, was highly unusual. She became a funeral junkie, attending any memorial service in the region, whether she knew the deceased or not. It was said that over the next 15 years, she missed not a single funeral within a 20-mile radius, often walking miles in all weathers to attend.

In late 1923, Albert Wise died suddenly and his wife's already bizarre behavior took a turn for the worse. She began wandering around after dark, often showing up at neighboring farms in the middle of the night, where she'd stand outside and howl like a dog. Roused from sleep, the occupants would find her standing in the yard, wild-eyed and foaming at the mouth.

Her strange behavior only abated when she found love again, with a farmhand from one of the neighboring ranches, named Walter Johns. But Martha's joy was short-lived. Walter was much younger than Martha and her family did not approve of the union. After a series of bitter quarrels with her mother, aunt and uncle, a heartbroken Martha eventually called off the relationship and Johns left town.

On Thanksgiving night, 1924, several of the Hasel clan woke with severe stomach cramps. All soon recovered, with the exception of Martha's 72-year-old mother, Sophie, whose condition steadily grew worse until she eventually died on December 17.

Then, after the 1925 New Year's celebration, Wise's uncle, Fred Gienke, his wife Lily, and six of their children, came down with severe stomach upsets and had to be hospitalized. Lily died in early January 1925, Fred on February 9.

Their deaths were attributed to gastroenteritis, but they weren't the only unusual events to occur around Hardscrabble during early 1925. Within weeks, a number of buildings, including a church, had been damaged by mysterious fires that appeared deliberately set. The sheriff launched an investigation and soon turned up an interesting clue. While tracking purchases of substances that might have been used as accelerants in the fires, he discovered that Martha Wise had been purchasing large quantities of arsenic.

It raised new questions about the deaths of Martha's relatives and an autopsy was ordered on Lily Gienke. Her stomach and intestines were found to contain substantial amounts of the poison.

Brought in for questioning, Martha initially denied any involvement in the deaths. Eventually, though, she broke down and confessed to poisoning the water buckets at her relative's homes. Seventeen family members were affected, three died, while several others were left permanently crippled.

Wise went on trial for the murder of Lily Gienke on May 4, 1925. Found guilty, she was sentenced to life in prison. She died there on June 28, 1971, at the age of 79.

David Leonard Wood

During 1987, a rash of disappearances of teenaged girls and young women had police in El Paso, Texas, baffled. Fourteen-year-old Marjorie Knox was the first to disappear, reported missing from nearby Chaparral, New Mexico, on February 14, 1987. Three weeks later, on March 7, Melissa Alaniz, 13, vanished without a trace from El Paso.

Desiree Wheatly, 15, was seen in the company of a heavily tattooed man before she disappeared in El Paso on June 7. Three days later, another woman was missing. At 20, Karen Baker was the oldest of the victims.

On June 28, 19-year-old Cheryl Vasquez-Dismukes vanished; five days later 17-year-old Angela Frausto was gone. Twenty-four-year-old Maria Casio failed to return home on August 19. Her car was found on August 21, but of Maria, there was no trace. A week later, on August 28, 14-year-old Dawn Smith left her El Paso home, never to be seen again.

By now, alarm bells were well and truly jangling at the El Paso Police Department. Eight young females missing without a trace within the space of seven months could mean only one thing. And yet, the police had no evidence of homicide. What they had was a batch of unsolved missing persons dockets.

That was to change on September 4, 1987, when utility workers unearthed Maria Casio's remains in the desert northwest of El Paso. The police were called and conducted a search of the immediate area, turning up Karen Baker in a shallow grave just 100 yards away. Both women appeared to have been strangled.

Another significant clue surfaced on September 22. On that day, a woman came forward and testified that in July 1987, she had been walking home from a convenience store in northeast El Paso when a man stopped and offered her a lift. The woman accepted, but rather than drive her to her apartment as he'd promised, the man had driven her out into the desert, where he tied her with a rope to the front of his truck. He then took a shovel out of the vehicle and walked a short distance away from the road, where he began digging a hole. Ten to fifteen minutes later, he returned, threw a "brownish red" blanket on the ground and began ripping her clothes off. Then he suddenly broke off the attack, claiming he heard someone approaching.

The man then drove her to another location where he forced her to undress, gagged her, and tied her to a bush. He then raped her. Immediately afterwards, the man again said he heard someone approaching. He hastily threw his belongings into the truck and sped away, leaving the woman naked in the desert. The woman hadn't initially reported the incident because she'd been terrified that the man would find her.

El Paso PD detectives listened to her account with interest, especially as the tattooed man she described closely matched the man seen in the company of Desiree Wheatly, and several of the other missing girls. They asked the woman to lead them to the sites where she'd been assaulted. The first was in the same area where Maria Casio and Karen Baker had been discovered.

On October 20, 1987, hikers found the decomposed remains of Desiree Wheatly and Dawn Smith. Two weeks later, Angela Frausto was found nearby, interred in a shallow grave. (Marjorie Knox, Melissa Alaniz, and Cheryl Vasquez-Dismukes have never been found.)

The police meanwhile had a suspect in the case. Based on the description given to them by the woman who had escaped, investigators focused their attention on an ex-con named David Leonard Wood. Wood had previously served time for the attempted rape of a 12-year-old girl and for the rape of two other teens. He'd been paroled in January 1987 and had arrived in El Paso just days before the series of disappearances began.

Picked up for questioning, Wood vehemently denied any involvement in the murders, even though there was strong physical and circumstantial evidence connecting him to the crimes. He was also less than candid with his cellmates while awaiting trial, bragging openly about the killings. Those loose words would later come back to haunt him.

Donald Leonard Wood was found guilty on multiple counts of first-degree murder. On January 14, 1993, he was sentenced to die by lethal injection. That sentence was carried out on August 20, 2009.

Robert Zarinsky

Born in Linden, New Jersey, in 1941, Robert Zarinsky showed early signs of mental instability. Like many serial killers, he was a torturer of animals who particularly liked chopping the wings and heads off live birds. As he grew older, Zarinsky turned his cruel intentions to his younger sister, once beating her so badly that she missed three weeks of school. Far from discouraging this, his mother Veronica (who doted on Robert) merely advised him not to hit his sister in the face, so as not to leave marks.

With that kind of parental guidance, it is hardly surprising that Zarinsky grew to be a young thug. By his early teens, he was the leader of a street gang, specializing in burglaries and muggings. These hoodlums also preyed on local merchants by demanding "protection money." Even Zarinsky's father, Julius, who owned a fresh produce store was not immune. Zarinsky demanded the full take from the store, giving his father only a $5 per week "allowance." He also enjoyed humiliating Julius in public, rubbing tomatoes in his face while his gang sniggered in the background.

On November 28, 1958, Zarinsky and his cousin, Theodore Schiffer, were burglarizing a Pontiac dealership in Rahway, New Jersey, when they were confronted by police officer Charles Bernoskie. A scuffle ensued, during which Bernoskie was fatally wounded. The murder would remain unsolved until 1999 when Zarinsky's sister Judith Sapsa eventually testified to it. Zarinsky and Schiffer were both wounded in the incident, she said, and her mother had removed the bullets for them.

Inevitably, Zarinsky did fall foul of the law. Convicted in 1962, for torching five lumberyards and for desecrating 1,500 headstones at the Rosedale-Linden Cemetery, he was sent to Trenton State Psychiatric Hospital. In true sociopathic style, Zarinsky was able to dupe the state psychiatrists into giving him the all clear after just 13 months. By 1964, he was back on the streets of Linden.

On October 25, 1969, 16-year-old, Rosemary Calandriello disappeared. Calandrriello had last been seen sitting in a Ford motor vehicle matching the one owned by Zarinsky. Her body was never found.

At around the same time, the body of 16-year-old Linda Balbanow was fished from the Raritan River in Middlesex County. Linda had vanished in April, while walking from her job at a drug store in Union County, New Jersey. She'd been bludgeoned to death with a ballpeen hammer, similar to the one the police found in Zarinsky's car when they questioned him about Rosemary Calandriello's disappearance. Years later, hair found on the hammer would be forensically matched to Balbanow.

In 1974, the bodies of Doreen Carlucci, 14, and Joanne Delardo, 15, were found in Monmouth County. Both girls had been raped, beaten and strangled with lengths of electrical cable, which were still knotted around their necks. The police strongly suspected Zarinsky but lacked sufficient evidence to make an arrest.

They did, however, have enough proof to prosecute Zarinsky for the Calandriello murder. Zarinsky had apparently been bragging to acquaintances that he'd never be tried in the absence of a body. He was dead wrong on that score. Arrested in February 1975, he was found guilty in April and sentenced to life in prison.

A subsequent trial, in 2001, for the murder of Charles Bernoskie, resulted in an acquittal. But by 2008, prosecutors were ready to bring fresh murder charges against Zarinsky when DNA evidence linked him to the death of yet another teenaged girl.

Thirteen-year-old Jane Durrua had disappeared on the evening of Monday, November 4, 1968, after she took a shortcut through a field near her home in East Keansburg New Jersey. Her strangled corpse was found the next morning in a field in North Middletown.

The matter would never come to trial. Robert Zarinsky died on November 28, 2008, at South Woods State Prison in Bridgeton, New Jersey. His death was attributed to pulmonary fibrosis, a scarring of the lung tissue that makes breathing increasingly difficult.

50 American Monsters You've Probably Never Heard Of Volume 3

For more True Crime books by Robert Keller please visit

http://bit.ly/kellerbooks

Printed in Poland
by Amazon Fulfillment
Poland Sp. z o.o., Wrocław